NICHE MAR
AS A RURAL
DEVELOPMENT STRATEGY

ORGANISATION FOR ECONOMIC CO-OPERATION AND DEVELOPMENT

ORGANISATION FOR ECONOMIC CO-OPERATION AND DEVELOPMENT

Pursuant to Article 1 of the Convention signed in Paris on 14th December 1960, and which came into force on 30th September 1961, the Organisation for Economic Co-operation and Development (OECD) shall promote policies designed:

— to achieve the highest sustainable economic growth and employment and a rising standard of living in Member countries, while maintaining financial stability, and thus to contribute to the development of the world economy;

— to contribute to sound economic expansion in Member as well as non-member countries in the process of economic development; and

— to contribute to the expansion of world trade on a multilateral, non-discriminatory basis in accordance with international obligations.

The original Member countries of the OECD are Austria, Belgium, Canada, Denmark, France, Germany, Greece, Iceland, Ireland, Italy, Luxembourg, the Netherlands, Norway, Portugal, Spain, Sweden, Switzerland, Turkey, the United Kingdom and the United States. The following countries became Members subsequently through accession at the dates indicated hereafter: Japan (28th April 1964), Finland (28th January 1969), Australia (7th June 1971), New Zealand (29th May 1973) and Mexico (18th May 1994). The Commission of the European Communities takes part in the work of the OECD (Article 13 of the OECD Convention).

Publié en français sous le titre :

DES CRÉNEAUX COMMERCIAUX POUR UNE STRATÉGIE DE DÉVELOPPEMENT RURAL

Foreword

Rural areas abound in natural, traditional and cultural resources. Many of these would have market value if innovative rural entrepreneurs could tap their potential. New business opportunities utilising rural resources have expanded as lifestyles and consumer preferences have changed and diversified. Increased discretionary income and leisure time allow more people to spend time in the countryside, to participate in outdoor activities and to enjoy the products which only rural areas can provide.

OECD countries offer many examples of resource-based niche market activities often based on either an innovative idea or artisans' work, creating local quality and speciality products. Niche markets seek means of differentiating products from those of other competitors. In many cases, niche market activities can synergize business opportunities if they are well linked to service sectors, such as tourism. Their effects on the rural economy are positive, in particular for those areas where communities are small and other business opportunities are scarce.

This report consists of both theoretical discussion and empirical evidence. The empirical evidence is drawn from six case studies provided by OECD countries. Each case study illustrates different niche goods or service activities categorised according to resource base, such as natural resources, traditional and cultural heritage, or environment and amenity resources. Although the report highlights many elements necessary for niche market development, it is by no means exhaustive, but serves to underline the need to take into account the different contexts of development in rural areas.

At its sixth session in June 1994, the Group of the Council on Rural Development recommended that in view of its interest, the work on niche markets done to date should be made more widely known, and therefore this report be published on the responsibility of the Secretary-General of the OECD.

Table of Contents

Chapter 1
Defining Niche Markets

Chapter 2
Summary of Case Studies in Member Countries

Chapter 3
Key Elements for Success – Provisional Conclusions

Appendix
Case Studies

List of Boxes

List of Figures

List of Maps

List of Tables

Executive Summary

The case studies reviewed in this report provide good examples of how resources which are often overlooked or under-utilised can provide new or expanded opportunities for employment and income creation in rural areas. The enterprises they describe produce goods or services drawing on special natural resources, skills, or heritages that are specific to their community or region. They document the creation of new jobs for women, farmers, cultural minorities, and the whole range of rural populations for whom new employment opportunities are essential. The precise magnitude of their effects on local employment and income is not documented in most of the cases, but even a small number of new jobs may be significant in a rural setting. Moreover, comparatively small successes can have important indirect consequences, inspiring emulation, building morale and social cohesion, and increasing the skills of the workforce, as many of these cases illustrate.

The case studies identified nine elements, most of which are present to one degree or another in all the cases, and appeared necessary to create the successful niche market business. The combined list includes both endogenous actions and externally provided assistance. One is a careful local assessment of available resources. Another is finding and building on a competitive advantage, which in rural areas often requires local initiative, entrepreneurship, and partnerships. The third element is the organisational structure among the local people for new business. The fourth element is territorial linkage. The fifth is advertising, important in all the cases. The establishment of information and communication networks for production and/or marketing purposes is the sixth element. Seventh, in every case some externally provided technical and/or financial assistance was identified as essential. Eighth, in some cases an appropriate regulatory regime was critical. Lastly, a periodic re-evaluation of the activity to make sure it stays on the right track in rapidly changing circumstances was deemed critical to success.

Two patterns are evident in the descriptions. Some of the activities are small in scale, carried out by a specific enterprise, and focused on a single skill or product. Others, usually those planned regionally, are part of an integrated strategy for the development of some unit of territory, community or region. The objective of the latter is to establish the territory as a niche to which traditional goods and new services, especially in the rapidly growing tourism sector, are linked.

At the outset, this report explored the definition of niche markets from the perspectives of marketing and economic theory, and what is known of modern consumer behaviour. Classically, niche products target market segments and compete partly on the basis of price. No examples of classical niche goods and services, which meet the most rigorous theoretical tests, are found in the case studies.

The enterprises described in these cases diverge from the classic strategy, mostly seeking to create a competitive advantage through product differentiation by identification of the products with a specific territory and its attributes – landscape, scenery, culture, or historic monuments. There is little emphasis on targeting an identified market segment or competing on the basis of price.

Product differentiation is an accepted business practice, often a major objective of advertising. For firms, differentiation on the basis of a territorial identity is one of several options to enhance product competitiveness. But for the development of a rural community or region it has obvious advantages. The territory is used to promote the product, but the product also promotes the territory. This symbiosis can simultaneously increase the value of many local resources, especially high value agricultural products, traditional skills and outstanding natural or man made features, as attractions for tourism. Moreover, the types of activities linked with territory, as exemplified in the cases, tend to be labour-intensive. This is very desirable in rural areas where job opportunities are in short supply. And since labour costs are already relatively low in such areas, cost reductions which might be necessary in a classic niche market strategy could be self-defeating for development, if not impossible in practice. However, there is insufficient evidence in this study to suggest that territorial differentiation is the only approach to niche market activities in rural areas. There also may be more classical examples.

Given the apparent success of the activities described and what has been learned about the endogenous and externally provided elements regarded as necessary for success, the most important question is not the degree to which they are properly called niche market activities. More important is how rural development strategies can facilitate and encourage the creative use of local resources as exemplified in these case studies.

The government measures which the studies suggest can encourage niche market activities clearly fall within the policy framework developed by the Group of the Council on Rural Development.[1] In addition to a sound general economic climate, the basic policies recommended by the Group include an economy oriented to the market; modest measures to improve communication and transportation technologies, giving rural people better access to information and markets; and environmental resource inventories to help community leaders and entrepreneurs identify local assets available and appropriate for development. The case studies clearly re-affirm the importance of such measures.

For more remote and intermediate rural areas, the Group assigned priority to policies directed at the development of human and natural resources and to measures to facilitate economic diversification and structural adjustment. It specifically mentioned technical assistance, training, and the research and exploration of economic spheres in which rural areas have a comparative advantage, including markets for niche products. The case studies revealed the existence of many such policies and illustrate their value in supporting niche market activities.

Suggestions for action in individual communities are necessarily general. At the local level, how best to include a niche market business in a rural development strategy depends on factors such as the size of the economy, the cohesiveness of the community and the opportunities for alternative uses for available resources. In a very small rural economy, a single niche market activity might be the core of development, and promoting this business, the heart of a development strategy. In a larger target area, a similar activity might be one among several components in a development scheme. But no matter how good the idea, it is unlikely that it can be successfully imposed from above; at the local level, a critical factor is the involvement and contribution of individuals.

Niche market activities, as the name implies, are focused on economic activities in the market-place. For many reasons, including the promotion of structural adjustment in the agriculture sector and the importance of maintaining a territorial balance of economic opportunities, the desirability of certain forms of government assistance in establishing new enterprises in rural areas is generally accepted, so long as that assistance is not market distorting over the long run. The nature of policies that provide non-distorting assistance has been discussed by the OECD Committees for Industry and Agriculture in so far as market propriety and transparency are concerned.[2] Any measures to promote niche market activities should take into account the long-run market viability of these activities.

Although the economic effects of the niche market activities on the local economies are obviously positive, case studies alone do not provide sufficient evidence to support firm conclusions on several important questions. For example, are there many other, less successful, attempts made to create niche businesses? How do the costs and benefits of these cases compare with other options which might have been chosen? How large is the market for the kinds of goods and services that are being provided? If the approach is copied, will demand quickly fall behind supply?

Introduction

Despite their many positive attributes, rural areas in OECD countries are most often described with terms such as: declining economies, depopulation and low capital investment. The problems of scarce employment opportunities, low incomes, poor services, ageing populations and deteriorating environments are widely known. The cause is mostly decades of structural changes in rural economies, exacerbated by the misallocation of resources in efforts to avoid or impede adjustment to those changes. Over-investment in some sectors, particularly agriculture, has not only hindered structural adjustment, but also diverted local populations from turning to other opportunities, effectively closing the door on alternative activities. Key assets of rural areas are being wasted in missed opportunities, while at the same time taxpayers are bearing increasingly heavy burdens to compensate for the social consequences.

While sharing certain problems, rural areas vary significantly among OECD countries and within each country. They have different geographical, environmental, historical and cultural attributes. Exogenous factors such as global trends, diverse national economic performance, and technological change also exert influences on rural areas, making economic and social patterns even more complex. In the past, the features that characterise rural areas often have been thought of as bottlenecks to development and largely ignored in the development process. Evidence of their neglect can be found in the disappearance of locally distinct products and loss of the traditional skills and knowledge used in producing them, untapped environmental resources and amenities, and the absence of measures for the preservation of cultural and natural heritages.

There is a growing belief that rural populations should no longer underrate the features which make them unique. Rather, they should at least consider local specialties and resources as potential advantages for development and at the same time as sources of local pride. The value the entire society places on rural areas is changing, partly as the result of an overall increase in leisure time and income. There is a growing interest in outdoor recreation, nature, health and quality of life which many rural areas offer. Changes in consumer tastes and preferences have increased demand for goods and services which are in some way special and out of the ordinary. Advanced technology has encouraged the growth of this demand in some ways. This situation appears to have created new business opportunities that utilise the resources of many rural areas. The question is how best to exploit these resources for successful rural development.

There are many experiences in OECD countries which shed light on exactly this question. Various businesses have been established in rural areas building on special local resources. They often demonstrate an intelligent use of untapped resources. They are diverse in terms of their scale, the distribution of their benefits and their effects on the economy. Some of them are unique to the area and have been developed to cater to a small and specific segment of the market. Their activities include the production of traditional and quality goods and the provision of services for sport and recreation. In other cases, an area simply benefits from its favourable environment and the amenities it can offer, attracting new enterprises of various kinds as well as new residents. Both cases have tangible and intangible effects on the local community and its economy which are not negligible. These businesses supply what are called "niche markets" with "niche goods and services" and the purpose of this study is to explore their scope and understand more clearly the economic principles that define them.

Evidence in OECD countries suggests that "niche markets" and the activities to satisfy those markets have positive implications for rural development, creating employment opportunities, encouraging entrepreneurship and strengthening social cohesion. They contribute to the structural adjustment of the rural economy through income diversification. In spite of this evidence, little attempt has been made to study the elements and policies which make such markets work and how they can be adopted and promoted as part of rural development strategies. This study takes a heuristic approach, using the experiences in selected case studies from OECD countries to identify common features and differences, and to develop hypotheses rather than final conclusions.

The remainder of the main report consists of three chapters, which are highlighted in the Executive Summary. Chapter 1 explores the definition of niche markets from the perspectives of both marketing and economic theory, and in light of what is known of consumer behaviour. Chapter 2 explains how the case studies were selected and the various aspects examined. It provides a short summary of each case, and makes observations on important elements in each. In Chapter 3, key factors identified in the case studies for successful niche market businesses are discussed and provisional conclusions are drawn.

14

Chapter 1

Defining Niche Markets

The term "niche market" is now used widely, but imprecisely. The result is a good deal of misunderstanding and confusion. Before exploring the case studies, it is useful to review marketing, economic, and consumer behaviour theory to clarify the key concepts. In marketing, a niche market is often discussed in terms of strategies of product differentiation and market segmentation. In economics it is explained in terms of the theories of imperfect competition, utility and elasticity. Marketing strategy is strongly influenced by economics, which has a long history of research into product differentiation in association with such subjects as monopolistic competition and optimal diversification of products. Consumer behaviour also plays an important role, especially consumer choice and tastes, psychology, and other elements in the purchasing process. All these factors will be discussed in an attempt to clarify the meaning of the concept "niche market".

Marketing Considerations

In discussing niche markets, strategies of product differentiation and market segmentation are often confused with one another, though they are quite distinct. Schnaars[3] explains both strategies clearly in his basic marketing text, on which the following discussion draws.

Product Differentiation: Many products sell on image as well as physical attribute. A strategy of differentiation, as the term implies, is concerned with making the tangible and intangible aspects of a product different from those offered by other sellers. ...Product differentiation takes a competitor orientation, but it also provides consumer benefits. On the supply side, it allows firms to minimise competition and earn higher profits. On the demand side, it provides consumers with a greater variety of goods and services.

Examples of advertising which stress some special feature of a product of a certain brand – to establish differentiation – abound. Its objective is to persuade the consumer that the brand is superior in a particular aspect, usually quality, function, design, or service support.

Market Segmentation: Segmentation relies on specialisation. It does not seek to satisfy all consumers. Instead, it provides something special to a small, but defensible part of the market. ...Segmentation avoids competition across a broad market by focusing on part of the market. It appeals especially to consumers in that segment with either lower prices or unique products, which are designed specifically for them. ...Segments are formed in one of two ways: a) they either exist naturally in a market, to be discovered by astute marketers, or b) they are created by marketers who see an opportunity. Unlike differentiation, segments are not solely the creation of marketers.

Examples include sporting goods specifically for baseball, baby carriages and ethnic cuisine.

A pure niche market is a market segment: small, narrow and specific. Product differentiation strategies can, however, help to create a niche or segment; indeed, most niches in the market depend, more or less, on this strategy. Technological advances can facilitate market segmentation through differentiation. For example, a car equipped with a set of accessories such as sunroof, stereo, wireless telephone, ice-cooler and wide seats, is designed to address a limited but specific segment of consumers who value convenience in addition to mechanical performance.

How does a firm differentiate its products from others and so create a segment in the market? In marketing strategies competitive advantage is used to answer this question. As Porter[4] argues, *"Competitive advantage is at the heart of a firm's performance in the competitive market. ...It stems from the many discrete activities a firm performs in designing, producing, marketing, delivering, and supporting its products. Each of these activities can contribute to a firm's relative cost position and create a basis for differentiation."* By producing differentiated products which may appeal to specific segments of the market a firm can strengthen its competitiveness. One product differentiation strategy is to improve quality to such a degree that the product is no longer just better, but qualitatively different. This may involve combining several elements such as superior design and style, and greater reliability and durability. Consumer perceptions of quality may also be transferred to a brand, which comes to be identified with quality.

Not all market segments are created by producers. They also may exist as latent demand; consumers may be prepared to buy something with a particular mix of qualities, independent of the existence of a product known to meet their desires. There are undiscovered, untapped niche markets for new products or very high quality versions of an existing product. In addition to the tangible components of product quality mentioned above, quality is also a matter of the perceptions, values and tastes of consumers. Consumers often make a quality distinction on the basis of whether a product is mass- or custom-produced, and between products containing different combinations of quality elements.

A successful (niche) segmentation strategy has several advantages for producers; a firm can reduce the intensity of competition by targeting and securing a defensible segment in the market. In doing so, it can virtually exclude substitute products of new entrants. However, this strategy also has risks in a competitive market. These narrow markets are often vulnerable to the changes in taste and demand. And if demand grows

Box 1. What is quality? Concepts of quality, and their direct and indirect components

Concept	Direct	Indirect
Self-evident	Something which does not appear to get in anywhere else.	Quality which other people's children would benefit from. May overlap with others.
Inspector's quality	Amalgam of other people's quality. Self-evident.	Quality of Pressure groups taken into account.
User-based	Product lines producing satisfactions. Different products meeting the same satisfactions. One product line meeting different satisfactions.	Ecological factors benefit others.
Buyer-based	Buyer buys for several users. Buyer gets satisfaction from good buy, being seen to be good home-maker, keeping family happy, and so on.	Buyer combines wants of users, some of whom have no financial constraints.
Distributor quality	Prestige goods. No shrinkage, no waste, good shelf life. Low handling costs, low floor, shelf space requirements. Takes rough handling. High margin.	Fast turnover/high margin, both deriving from buyer's quality and, less directly, users'.
Production-based	Meets specifications. Low product costs, high yields, few outgrades, low pest and disease incidence, not dangerous or unpleasant.	Sells easily at a good price deriving from distributors' quality, and from buyers' and users'.
Input-based	None.	Quality and value determined by its use to producers.
Product-based	?	?

and profits increase beyond a certain point, mass marketers may find new ways to enter the market and compete.

Economic Considerations

Economic literature suggests that most markets are imperfectly competitive; firms are not always price takers, and entry into a market is rarely totally unrestricted. In imperfect markets, firms produce differentiated products to compete with others. Prices reflect some product characteristics and sometimes a firm has latitude in determining prices. Taking the example of soap, as described by Lipsey *et. al.*:[5] *"One firm's soap might be similar to another firm's soap, but it differs in chemical composition, colour, smell, softness, brand name, reputation, and a host of other characteristics that matter to customers. This is the phenomenon of product differentiation. It implies that each firm has a certain degree of local monopoly power over its own product. It could raise its price, even if its competitors did not, and not lose all of its sales."* However, in actual markets, the price elasticity of demand is usually rather high because close substitutes exist in the market.

As the market for soap illustrates, the basis for consumer choices differ. They vary according to preferences, disposable income, and the availability of substitutes. Dickson *et. al.*[6] point out that, *"under the condition of demand heterogeneity, it may be possible to view the total market as a set of submarkets or segments, with each having its demand determined by a unique segment's demand function."* This view of the market as a series of demand curves, each representing a separate market segment seeking a different product, is illustrated in the Figure 1 below. Since a niche market is a specific type of market segment, even for relatively heterogeneous products there may be potential for one or more niche markets.

The economic principle of utility is often referred to in explaining why consumers are willing to pay a little more for a good or service which they value highly and which

Figure 1. **Demand curves representing market aggregation and segmentation**

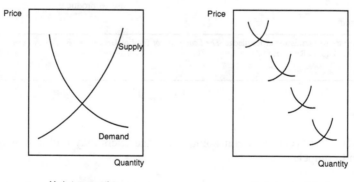

Market aggregation

Market segmentation

"The object of market aggregation is to fit the market to the product. Market Segmentattion is an attempt to fit the product to the market."

Source: Fundamentals of Marketing, W.J. Stanton, *et. al.*, 1991.

corresponds to their tastes and preferences. Utility is generally defined as satisfaction (or subjective value) which an individual obtains or derives from consuming a certain good or service. Marginal utility denotes the additional satisfaction derived from consuming one additional unit. Facing a choice of goods and services, consumers are assumed to attempt to increase their satisfaction by allocating their expenditures to maximise utility. It is assumed that after acquiring necessities, consumers will spend their discretionary income (and time) on brand or quality products rather than mass produced commodities. As the marginal utility for such products is higher, consumers are prepared to pay a higher price to obtain a little more.

Theoretically, in a perfectly competitive market the price of a product is determined through the interplay of supply and demand. The price is an important indicator in the consumer buying process. Since there are no differences between homogeneous products except for price, consumers will chose the least expensive. In an imperfect market, however, prices alone do not determine the consumer's choice. As mentioned, differentiation may be a more important factor to consumers than price. Moreover, uncertainty caused by limited knowledge or product information may lead a consumer to buy a brand name, high quality, and possibly niche product chiefly to increase confidence and security. Successful product differentiation can thus produce a price premium, the degree of which may depend on supply and demand functions. It is likely to reap the highest premium when competition is limited and the market is most segmented, as in the case of niche markets.

Consumer Behaviour

Analysis of consumer behaviour is an important element in a marketing strategy. Consumers have various strategies for making purchasing decisions, especially when buying something for the first time. They sometimes buy impulsively, of course. The many theories of consumer behaviour are a mix of economic, sociological, psychological and behavioural analyses. One model[7] includes: need recognition, choice of involvement level (a decision about the time and effort to invest in the remaining processes), identification of alternatives, evaluation of alternatives, decision to buy, and post-purchase behaviour. The degree of involvement in each aspect of the process depends on the consumer's perceptions, personal circumstances, and information on the products which they are considering. Different groups of people, classified by demography, income, personality and other factors have different buying behaviours. These differences create discrete segments in the market.

Consumer behaviour varies in response to changes in income, life-style and improvements in technologies. A growing number of people now seek individualised products, or something in some way different from what is easily available to others. They find the differences they seek in the quality, scarcity and novelty of products. This trend stems not just from the availability of a wide range of products, but results from the consumer's own motivations and perceptions. Motives for purchasing often include establishing a certain self-identity or prestige. Perceptions of how products serve these

Box 2. People's tastes are diversifying!

Consumer's tastes are changing. More and more consumers are buying goods and services tailor-made to their particular needs. This type of consumer behaviour has created the production of goods and services which are custom made. For example, in department stores the availability of custom-made goods such as women's shirts, lingerie and even sundry goods have increased sales. In the *T* car company, 60% of total car sales are for customised cars. Consumers are also increasingly demanding that these goods be cheaper and rapidly available. This demand is being increasingly realised by combining artisan's skills and modern technology. One successful example is the "Pernasonic" bicycle by *M* Electric Inc. Its production process is unique: the customer's order from a bicycle shop is sent by FAX to the factory; based on this information the factory designs the bicycle using the CAD system with a combination of artisanal craftsmanship and industrial production. The "Pernasonic", which is very close to an artisanal product, satisfies the individual's specific demand, is produced in two weeks and sold for about 100 thousand yen.

Figure A. **Distribution of preferences in mass production and consumption**

Figure B. **Distribution of diversified preferences**

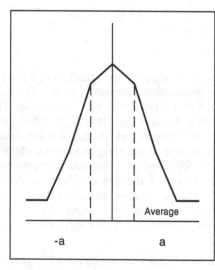

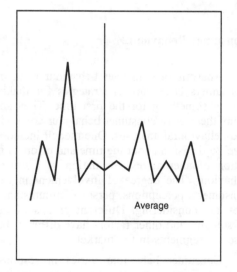

(continued on next page)

(continued)

The success of the "Pernasonic" depends on important information about the market. The physical data of the customer (*e.g.* lengths of arm and leg) is identified in a normal distribution curve (Figure A), while the psychological data (*e.g.* choice of model and colour) shows an irregular curve (Figure B). It used to be possible to mass produce a standard bicycle by knowing the average customer's tastes. In recent years, however, consumers' tastes have become more particular and fall in the same distribution curve as the choice of model and colour of the "Pernasonic". Foreseeing changes in the customised market will be difficult if one depends only on information for the average mass market consumer. Of significance is the recognition of the "desires and needs" of the consumer, and targeting the market through information from market leaders and innovators.

Source: Nippon Keizai Shinbun, 3rd March 1993, T. Ohashi.

objectives are important for choice, probably playing a basic role in the early stages of consumer decisions. This makes it even more difficult to anticipate consumer behaviour.

Market research is often undertaken to understand and predict consumer behaviour. The current approach usually includes detailed surveys profiling consumers' social, psychological and economic characteristics. The data are processed and analysed mathematically. This is not always useful, however, because markets change so quickly. The more competitive the market is, the more dynamic is consumer behaviour, and the less reliable is this form of market research. Recent markets are said to be "consumer driven", which means very sensitive to consumers' needs and tastes. Consumer behaviour in these markets is not easily anticipated. However, it is clear that diverse and undiscovered needs offer the potential for numerous and varied new products and strategies. Differentiation and segmentation strategies based on innovative ideas rather than traditional market research may be the most direct path to the consumer.

Chapter 2

Summary of Case Studies in Member Countries

This section explains the criteria used in selecting actual examples of the marketing of niche goods and services in rural areas of OECD countries and the questions that provide the framework for examining the case studies. It summarises each case and makes observations on key elements.

Selection Criteria

Many activities in rural areas of OECD countries are described as the production of niche goods and services. Some probably meet the strictest definition of the term as it is discussed in Chapter 1; many do not. As suggested earlier, it is not easy to say whether a specific good or service is targeted to a genuine niche market, and even less so without specialised knowledge of the particular market. The literature also indicates that true market niches may appear and often disappear very rapidly. Indeed, offering what the producer hopes will become a niche good or service is one strategy to create a niche.

The case studies in this report were selected from among those presented by OECD countries. The criteria used in choosing the cases is described below. While good examples were sought, no test was applied to exclude "non-genuine" niche market cases. Given the complexity of isolating pure niche markets, excluding dubious cases would have required developing elaborate rules and either asking authorities to apply them or conducting "pre-studies" of each case. Either approach would have been costly and time consuming. It is unlikely that the results would have been definitive. Moreover, this study is less concerned with theory than with what can be learned from those who have sought to apply a niche strategy in rural areas.

Beginning with the assumption that the cases chosen are examples of marketing niche goods and services, this study examines the degree to which that is true in a technical sense, and at the same time it explores specific elements in each case. In selecting case studies, emphasis was given to finding examples of the production of goods or services that use resources characteristic of rural areas. The very fact that they use typically "rural resources" justifies some presumption that they have a special appeal to consumers and therefore are niche goods and services. At the same time it should yield

23

examples that are more generally useful to other rural areas. Characteristically "rural resources" were classified as: natural resources, tradition and cultural heritage, and environment and amenity resources. Because rural employment has traditionally been concentrated in the primary sector or manufacturing, while net employment growth is in the service sector in most countries, it was decided that an equal number of examples of niche services would be chosen. This creates a matrix (Table 1) with categories of "niche" goods or services as shown in the table below. The table also gives examples reported by OECD countries of niche goods and services in each category. Obviously, this is a suggestive, not a representative, sample.

The defining principles and a brief description of niche goods and services by category is given below.

Niche Goods I

Goods produced using the natural resources of rural areas, including value-added and processed agricultural, sea, forestry and mineral products. Examples:

Table 1. **Matrix of niche goods and services with examples**

| Niche | Resource element | | |
	Natural	Tradition and cultural heritage	Environment and amenity
Goods	[I] * High quality vegetables and fruits * Traditionally made cheeses * Organic produce * Medicinal plants * Local pickles * Dried flowers * Fish paste and dried fish * Mineral springs * Other agricultural, sea, or forest products	[II] * Crafts such as ceramics and pottery * Jewellery * Embroidery * Rugs * Wooden toys and bowls * Traditional costumes * Flax knits * Other goods produced by traditional skills	[III] * Attractive environments, good climate, clean air which may attract retirees for living, research centers and high technology enterprises * Goods produced by using local energy or scarce resources such as pure or mineral water
Services	[IV] * Tools, outfitters and guides for hunting, fishing, camping and skiing * Local hotels and inns * Local restaurants * Holiday farms * Ecological museums * Natural parks	[V] * Historical monuments * Traditional architecture * Local museums * Local festivals and folk dances * Restaurants serving traditional cuisine	[VI] * Holiday villages and rest homes * Heath and fitness centres * Conference and training centres equipped with accomodation facilities

Source: OECD Secretariat.

high-quality vegetables and fruits, organic produce, medicinal plants, cheeses, dried fish and flowers, and mineral water.

Niche Goods II

Goods are produced and marketed based on the historical or cultural attributes of the rural area usually developed using the resources and traditional skills of the local work force. Examples: cottage industries and crafts such as ceramics and pottery, jewellery, rugs embroidery, walking sticks, wooden toys, flax knits, and traditional costumes.

Niche Goods III

Goods are produced in rural areas with natural amenities (environmental goods) which provide an attractive environment for the relocation or creation of industries. Local natural resources and skills are not necessarily essential to the production of these goods but are considered advantageous. Examples: attractive environments, good climate and clear air which may attract research centres, high-technology enterprises, and industries capable of using local sources of energy or scarce resources such as pure water.

Niche Services IV

Services specific to the natural resources of the rural area, differentiating them from similar activities carried out elsewhere. They include recreational and tourist activities which make use of natural resources, such as farm holidays, fishing, canoe tours, hill-walking, camping, as well as other activities such as horse breeding. Natural parks, nature reserves and landscape management are included in this category, as are hotels and restaurants which support these activities or make use of local produce.

Niche Services V

Services for recreational and tourist activities based upon the traditions and cultural heritage of the area. Examples: historical monuments and local museums, traditional architecture, local festivals and folklore dances, and restaurants serving traditional cuisine.

Niche Services VI

Services which are not specific to the rural area but are created or developed there, making use of the natural amenities and the local environment. Examples:

health and fitness centres, rest homes and villages, and conference and training centres equipped with accommodation facilities.

Although most niche goods and services reported by OECD countries fall into one of these categories, the categories are not exhaustive. In addition, certain activities may fall into two or more categories, in a combination which might be still more effective in addressing a narrow market segment. A combination of natural resource goods and services, for example, might be mutually reinforcing and therefore even more competitive.

Elements Examined

In addition to a general description of the niche market activity and its context, the case studies were designed to provide information on the following four questions:

1. *What are the competitive advantages reflected in the niche market activity? How are competitive advantages enhanced?*
2. *What elements are indispensable to the success of the activity?*
3. *What are the effects of the niche market and its related activities on the local community and its economy?*
4. *How are niche market activities integrated in rural development strategies?*

Information stemming from these questions is the basis for an assessment of how the niche market concept works as a business device in the market; how its application contributes to local development by creating employment and income opportunities, and how the approach can be made part of a broader rural development strategy used by authorities at various levels.

The Cases

The case studies on which this study draws are:

Floriculture Using Local Energy	Japan	Niche Goods (I)
Traditional Handicrafts	Norway	Niche Goods (II)
Retirement Living in Elliot Lake	Canada	Niche Goods (III)
Ecological Tourism in the Amvrakikos Gulf	Greece	Niche Services (IV)
The Green Gold of Magnoac	France	Niche Services (V)
Holiday Village in Litschau	Austria	Niche Services (VI)

Summaries and Observations

The observations after each of the summaries in this section are based on the full case studies presented in Appendix. The summaries are carried out from the view point of elements examined mentioned above and provided for the convenience of the reader.

Box 3. Was the environment of importance to the migration decision?

What forces underlie this considerable migration flow of actual or potential business entrepreneurs to the countryside? The survey could not address this important topic in detail. But it does reveal that one, if not the major stimulus is the perceived environmental attractiveness of England's villages and rural areas as a place to live (Figure A). No less that four out of every five migrant founders in remote rural areas, and three quarters of those in accessible rural areas, reported that this was of "some" or "great" importance to their original migration decision. In contrast, the equivalent residential attractiveness of the urban areas surveyed was acknowledged as important by only 59% of the smaller total of urban migrants, with only 22% reporting it as being very important compared with 50% of remote rural migrants. This difference is statistically very significant, and exists despite the inclusion in the urban sample of many historic and very attractive medium-sized towns, such as York, Harrogate, Carlisle, Chester, Norwich, Cheltenham, Exeter and Oxford.

Source: Business Success in the Countryside: The Performance of Rural Enterprise, pp. 14-15, Department of the Environment, D. Keeble, P. Tyler, G. Broom, and J. Lewis, London HMSO, June 1992.

Migrant founders and environment attractiveness

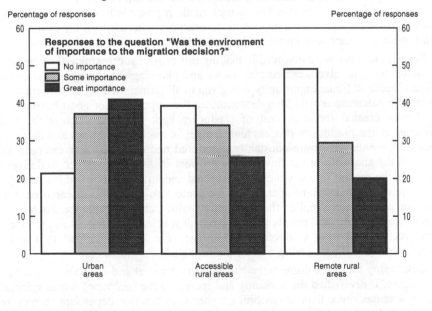

Floriculture Using Local Energy – Japan (Niche Goods I)

Amagase is a town in western Oita Prefecture, on the Island of Kyushyu. It is in a remote area; 80 per cent of its surface is mountainous. Agriculture is the major industry, with tourism based on a local hot spring resort, second. Like many rural areas, Amagase has suffered from loss of population, and those who remain are growing older. Twenty per cent of its people are over 65 years old. Its farmers, who each own an average of only 0.67 hectares of cultivated land, have suffered from the disadvantages of rice cultivation under unfavourable geographic conditions. Officials in Oita Prefecture have promoted the "Isson Ippin Undo" ("One Village-One Product") movement to counteract the problems common to its rural areas. A group of farmers in Amagase, with local governmental help, have undertaken floriculture (roses) using local energy from the hot spring as an "Isson Ippin Undo". With hot water from the spring, locally supplied energy allows year-round, low cost rose production, for which there is strong market demand. The shift from rice production to floriculture also contributed to structural adjustment in agriculture in this case.

The Amagase case study describes two major competitive advantages for the town; one is the strong partnership of local people and government, and the other is the new use of a local resource. Local leaders made persistent, patient efforts to encourage conservative farmers to change from rice production to floriculture. Several new associations were established and many meetings were held, first to involve and persuade local farmers, then to devise and carry out growing strategies, as well as strategies for acquiring necessary new facilities and marketing the roses. The second competitive advantage, the use of low cost local energy (the hot spring), made it possible to grow roses throughout the year, providing a cost advantage over competitors who used oil for heating in cold months when roses are at a premium in the market.

Several elements were involved in making this project successful. All of the relevant local actors were involved, exchanging views and planning the strategy for overcoming barriers to success. Equal opportunity was given to all farmers willing to participate in the project. The Amagase project also demonstrates the importance of good business skills. Associations created for each unit of producers kept in close touch with technical innovations in the production process and changes in market conditions and demand. All aspects of the enterprise were constantly monitored and evaluated. For example, taking account of the short life of cut flowers, the growers of Amagase learned to deliver their products to the market in lots which are inspected and strictly controlled for quality. The floriculture experiment centre operated by the prefecture conducted research on floriculture using heating, and supplied the associations with technical guidance. Such complete co-operation between local people and government was a major element in the success of the project as well as a competitive advantage. The process helped to foster both entrepreneurship and partnership among the farmers.

Developing the floriculture niche had important social and economic consequences for Amagase. It diversified the economy and increased the income of farmers; income is now, on average, more than seven times higher than the rice dependent income in the past. For the Amagase agricultural co-operative (Noukyou), shifting from rice production to floriculture and other cash crops increased total sales of agriculture products to

1 420 million yen in 1991, up from 980 million yen in 1980. The association employed 25 new entrants, mostly returnees from urban centres. At the same time it provided new employment opportunities for women. Diversification also promoted structural adjustment in agriculture, overcoming limits on arable land by consolidating holdings for new farming facilities.

The "Isson Ippin Undo" rural development strategy used in the Amagase case combined limited government assistance with local initiatives. It encouraged endogenous development based on innovative use of local resources. Local people were, however, constrained by limited financial resources. A questionnaire showed that area's first priority in terms of help from the government was for grants or long-term, low interest loans. For facilities that were to be used collectively, farmers in Amagase received government assistance from the Agricultural Structure Improvement Programme. The Amagase case demonstrates the potential of a rural development programme that combines local initiatives in partnerships with government expertise to foster genuinely endogenous development.

Traditional Handicrafts – Norway (Niche Goods II)

Promotion of the niche business of handicraft production throughout rural Norway is the subject of this case study. Rather than focusing on a single rural area, it discusses Norway Crafts, an agency created to help three groups of handicraft producers throughout country. The groups are local people in economically stagnant areas, farmers who need to supplement their incomes, and ethnic minorities. The first group includes people who live in small settlements in sparsely populated areas which have depended on currently diminishing government sponsored service employment. They produce many handicrafts which reflect the local culture and often adapt traditional products to new forms or shapes. The second group is farmers who need supplemental income to remain in the sector. These part-time farmers also produce various local crafts. The ethnic minorities (the Sami or Lappish people) produce "duodji" handicrafts. Mostly decorative objects and purses made of hides and wood, duodji are part of the long-standing cultural heritage of these ethnic groups. This case stresses how handicraft production contributes to maintaining local identity and heritage, while aiding economic development.

The competitive advantage shown in this case is in the traditional skills and knowledge needed to produce particular handicrafts, as well as the specific linkage of the craft products to rural Norway. But as the case also illustrates, only when they are used in concert with basic business skills can their full economic benefit be realised. Handicraft businesses have traditionally existed all over Norway. Carried out with skills which are passed down through generations, they produce many items with unique local or cultural associations. Local people create their own niche market when they sell special handicraft products, but the economic value to individuals and communities depends on other factors such as marketing activities and information networks. In this case, the change from isolated production activities to membership in a network which provides technical assistance and larger scale marketing is probably more important than the competitive advantage of the craftsmanship itself.

If craft production in rural Norway is to serve as an engine of development, the indispensable element appears to be better information for producers. Marketing strategies and information on other business related subjects have posed difficulties for traditional handicraft operations because they are typically small-scale enterprises in geographically isolated areas, and sometimes otherwise disadvantaged. Even though the production of traditional handicrafts may appear to be largely independent from external economic considerations, wider economic forces exert important influences, especially on the demand for their products. Norway Crafts, a trust programme supported by the government, seeks to increase employment opportunities in handicraft businesses and other small scale industries across Norway. It undertakes a variety of activities for collecting and providing information related to handicraft business development, including design, production, marketing, and distribution. It encourages joint ventures and new investment, and sometimes helps arrange financing. The Norway Crafts programme aims to create 2 000 new jobs by the end of the century, though not all in handicraft firms.

The impact of the programme is difficult to assess. No figures are available on its total effects on increasing employment or income. Nevertheless, the effects on people and communities are reportedly positive. These businesses draw on rural resources, especially human resources – people who have traditional skills and knowledge. Selling "duodji", for example, helps establish the identity of the local culture and the value of its traditions through trade with other parts of the economy. Another important benefit has been an increase in employment opportunities for women, for whom job opportunities are lacking in many rural areas. Better production and marketing of niche goods has also reportedly increased the involvement of women in the economic and cultural activities of some communities.

Although handicraft businesses are often small and thus limited in their direct employment effects, their value is multiplied when they are linked to other service sectors such as tourism. There are linkages to agriculture, forestry, local culture, and multiple-craft products as well. The increasing business sophistication of local producers, which comes from participation in information and marketing networks established by Norway Crafts, increases the longer term capacity for entrepreneurship as well.

Retirement Living in Elliot Lake – Canada (Niche Good III)

Elliot Lake is located 600 km north of Toronto, in northern Ontario and has earned a reputation as a "Jewel in the Wilderness". The community is surrounded by natural beauty; a hilly terrain with an abundance of trees and fresh air, providing natural amenities for its inhabitants. Since the establishment of a uranium industry in 1953, the city's economy has depended solely on mining. As a consequence, Elliot Lake has suffered from large movements in population due to the boom and bust cycle inherent in being a single industry town and the changing demand for its product. At the beginning of the nineties the uranium industry was declared redundant in Elliot Lake, causing a surplus of rental housing as the mining population began to leave the community. In 1987, however, the community adopted The Retirement Living concept to promote Elliot Lake as an affordable, beautiful, and pleasant place for retirees, and created The Non Profit Senior Housing of Elliot Lake Corporation to manage and promote the retirement community concept. By re-utilising the housing and infrastructure Elliot Lake has begun to diversify the local economy. Targeting the market segment of those fifty-five and over by offering low-priced quality housing with natural amenities, Elliot Lake has attracted retirees and seniors to live in the area. Such in-migration to date has produced a variety of economic and social benefits to Elliot Lake.

The community's initiatives to encourage the Retirement Living concept stemmed from the idea that if people with a disposable income who did not require employment could be enticed to live in Elliot Lake and occupy the empty housing units, the economy would cease to decline and the population base and the property values would begin to stabilise. This concept was generated by the challenge of boosting an economy in severe decline due to the closure of the mines and in the process, transforming a single sector economy into a more diversified one. There are two principal competitive advantages for the Elliot Lake Retirement Living concept. One is the availability of affordable, high quality housing, and the other is the natural amenities of the area, providing a quality of life and recreational activities suitable for seniors and retirees. Two of the major mining concerns "donated" housing to the Non Profit Senior Housing of Elliot Lake Corporation and in return received a tax credit for their contribution. This was a major advantage for Retirement Living as they owned the property outright with no debt and thus were able to provide a wide range of affordable housing to retirees. In addition, the small size of the community is favourable to retirees/seniors as it provides a strong sense of belonging and safety, both important issues to an elderly population.

The success in developing this market is due in large part to the competitive advantages mentioned the above, though there are other elements which are specific to this case. First, efforts have been taken to alter any adverse image of the area due to the uranium industry; advertising campaigns on Elliot Lake as a perfect place to live were run in newspapers, on television and radio, and brochures were distributed. In addition, a promotional caravan travelled throughout Ontario. Second, the technical and financial programmes sponsored by the local and provincial governments including special tax treatment for the seniors intending to move to Elliot Lake and public funding for training, renovation of housing units for the elderly and other programmes have contributed to the success of The Retirement Living concept. Third, the commitment and innovative thinking by community leaders contributed to the transformation of Elliot Lake's economy. The support of the Elliot Lake business community, the co-operation from the mining companies, and the creation of the Non Profit Senior Housing of Elliot Lake Corporation to promote the idea of a retirement community, all helped to revitalise the town's economy, and make Elliot Lake into an attractive location for seniors.

The effects of The Retirement Living programme on the community and economy of Elliot Lake are many. Over 3 000 retirees/seniors have moved to the area, since the beginning of the programme, helping to stabilise the population. As of November 1993 1 145 out of 1 600 available programme housing were occupied. Positive social effects are also visible: the influx of retirees has brought different skills and experiences into the area making possible a shift away from a transitory, "frontier town" mentality to one that is more rooted in a sense of heritage. Moreover, the programme has initially helped to maintain the service sectors in the community such as schools and hospitals. The effects on the local economy are more diverse with a shift to new businesses of in-home and home maintenance services such as security systems, handiwork and janitorial services. A rough calculation shows that 765 direct and indirect jobs have been created in the Elliot Lake area since the creation of the Retirement Living Programme.

The potential markets for the relocation of retirees/seniors in rural areas with natural amenities should increase in the future due to the growth in elderly populations. Although the Elliot Lake case is the product of a unique set of circumstances, such as an affordable housing stock and existing infrastructure set in beautiful natural surroundings, elements from this example could be repeated elsewhere. In adapting this programme to other areas, a smaller scale approach might be more feasible, such as utilising unoccupied housing and other available facilities. Moreover, this case signals the importance of the community's commitment to economic survival despite the death of its primary industry. In terms of the necessary complimenting policies, the case study suggests that an holistic approach in such programmes should be required to set goals and objectives for the economy and society in rural areas as a whole. The Elliot Lake example also highlights the fact that financial support including private investment is crucial for maintaining the necessary infrastructure.

Ecological Tourism in the Amvrakikos Gulf – Greece (Niche Services IV)

The wetland of Amvrakikos occupies the southern parts of Preveza and Arta Prefectures, covering a total area of about 130 km² and includes three large lagoons. Its ecological value stems from the uniqueness of the land form, rich halophilic and hydraulic vegetation, and diversity of its fauna. In the framework of the Amvrakikos Programme (of wetland protection), these flora and fauna assets are intended to be the object of a particular form of mild tourism, designed to harmonise environmental protection with the economic contributions of tourism. This is a version of "Eco-Tourism". With the help of government, local people are gradually developing this niche segment, avoiding placing excessive pressures on nature through tourism activities. This activity is still an experimental stage, but the strategy used in this case offers an approach to finding an appropriate market niche for valuable but fragile natural assets.

The Amvrakikos case suggests that an area's unique ecology can provide a competitive advantage and create a niche market. In this case that niche is a very special type of tourism – eco-tourism, but a market is not as yet clearly established, as the author notes. The Amvrakikos wetland offers several options for economic development including agriculture, aquaculture, and various types of tourism. A key question is the degree to which nature will support diverse economic activities without destroying the area's uniqueness, *i.e.* its ecological system with its rare flora and bird species.

Environmentally benign eco-tourism is a delicately balanced strategy, since it assigns equal priority to nature preservation and economic development. It requires a long process with many components. The findings of scientific studies are necessary to establish ecological boundaries; government regulations which zone wetlands and limit certain economic and recreational activities like hunting in key parts of the ecosystem also play a role. Identification of the necessary and appropriate services and facilities and the appropriate scale for housing and feeding tourists, is essential. Local people must be informed of opportunities and encouraged to provide such facilities. Certain small-scale public infrastructure (some provided in this case by the EC's LEADER programme) is also necessary. Many local people including farmers, fishermen, and entrepreneurs must be involved in various ways.

In the short term, this approach may not yield as much return as alternative strategies focused on agriculture, commercial fishing, or less carefully circumscribed tourism. However, in the long term, the eco-tourism strategy may the best way for this wetland area to realise its economic potential, while preserving its irreplaceable natural resources. Linking the Amvrakikos to limited tourism activities is a niche market strategy providing diverse economic opportunities for local people. Capitalising on the area's ecological integrity, scenic qualities, rare birds, and village festivals, local people will find entrepreneurial and employment opportunities from boat tours, seafood restaurants, local hotels, and the sale of locally produced products. Success will depend on the willingness of local people to accept the challenge of undertaking these new activities. Doing so will almost certainly provide them with a more promising economic future than the traditional sectors of the area.

Neither central nor regional government measures by themselves, nor local activities in isolation, no matter how important, are enough to develop an eco-tourism niche market in a territory as large as the Amvrakikos. An eco-tourism strategy requires a comprehensive rural-regional development effort built on contributions from both central and local governments and private partners. Such a region-wide approach, if it is successful, will use the niche market of eco-tourism as the basis for diversifying economic activities, providing alternative income sources for farmers and fishermen. The effects of such an extensive approach are particularly difficult to measure, though in this case there are some positive general results even in the early stages.

The Green Gold of Magnoac – France (Niche Services V)

Magnoac is in the north-eastern portion of the Department of the Hautes-Pyrénées, at the edge of the Gers and Haute-Garonne, in the foothills of the Pyrénées. It was sinking into recession when a mayor established a multipurpose association of the area's mayors to prepare a common development strategy. The area had long produced ducks, geese, and foie gras, but until recently had not processed them locally on a large scale. Since 1985 under the development plan, local people have been taking advantage of the area's tradition of high quality foie gras and related products which they are calling "the Green Gold of Magnoac" to establish a positive identity not only for local products, but for Magnoac itself. They have established local marketing and facility cooperatives with help from the department, the region, and the French government. They have expanded local foie gras production using a special, regionally distinct process. "Foie gras and its gastronomy" has been linked with tourism, appealing to nature-seeking tourists as well as to consumers of quality and traditional products. Production, and employment have grown steadily as has membership in the cooperatives. Morale in the area has profited. Between 1982 and 1990 the population in Magnoac stabilised and the average age fell.

Magnoac has used a combination of traditional and contemporary resources in its effort to establish a niche market for a special kind of tourism. Its resources include its reputation for gastronomy; its production of a high quality, high prestige food product; proximity to a large city and tourist traffic; and an attractive natural environment. Traditional skills in producing foie gras have been combined with a marketing campaign that seeks to differentiate its product and establish an identity for Magnoac for broader development purposes.

The establishment of local associations and cooperatives was a key element in the success of the project. The SIVOM (Syndicat Intercommunal à Vocation Multiple) played a catalytic role, especially in the initial stages of planning and building a local partnership. It also encouraged the creation of the CUMA (Coopérative d'Utilisation du Matériel Agricole) which was able to acquire the necessary facilities for processing and packing. The GIE (Groupement d'Intérêt Économique) which markets the products followed. These associations, built on local initiative and partnerships among producers and local governments, were supported financially, to varying degrees, by the central government, the region and the department.

The Magnoac project was specifically aimed at economic development in the tourism sector, but indirectly, first by developing and marketing goods to help establish the area's identity for tourism. As in most cases, it is difficult to specify the effects with precision. The marketing of locally produced foie gras has grown rapidly, 50 per cent per year. Women have been employed in duck and goose production. The number of producers belonging to the production co-operative has almost tripled. Farm income has increased. Consistent with the larger objective, local tourism is growing as well. A rural inn, 45 new gîtes, a campsite, and many other attractions have been established. Magnoac's population has stabilised; the number of empty buildings has fallen, as has the average age of the population. The project has also contributed to the social and cultural life of Magnoac, not only by preserving the territorial image of Magnoac and some of its distinctive features, but also by helping restore its economic destiny to its own people.

This project began as the conscious centre-piece of a locally based development strategy where the niche market activities comprise many aspects of development. Local people deliberately sought to combine traditional product and territorial images in mutually reinforcing ways to promote overall development of their area. To do so they organised themselves and marshalled local resources – those of the private sector, co-operatives, and local government. They also took advantage of various programmes offered by the region, the central government, and more recently, the EC.

Holiday Village in Litschau – Austria (Niche Services VI)

Litschau is a town in the Waldviertel region of Lower Austria, on the border of what is now the Czech Republic. Somewhat isolated by its geography and proximity to the Iron Curtain, until recently Litschau was heavily dependent on the textile industry. Since the early 1980's as that sector declined, Litschau faced several economic and social problems such as unemployment, out migration, and declining tax revenues. In response to this situation, Litschau decided to invest in tourism, a leading sector of the region's economy. The "Holiday Village" in Litschau is a community enterprise, linked to a more comprehensive regional tourism strategy which seeks to establish a distinct and authentic rural identity for the region as the most salubrious region of Austria. Its slogan is "Litschau – Countryside of Country Sights". The niche at which it aims is people who wish to spend their holidays or hold conferences in rural surroundings with a traditional cultural flavour. The scale of activities to establish this niche is large, seeking to integrate the Holiday Village with many related businesses which stress local cultural features. Local restaurants, for example, are encouraged to offer the traditional cuisine of the region. This case is

The solution to these problems (*i.e.* declining economic activities, lack of job, an ageing population, and the break-up of rural society) requires even greater determination than in urban areas to bring about a rural renaissance and achieve real local development. For successful development and job creation, rural areas are in desperate need of energetic and competent individuals, a thorough assessment and co-ordinated exploitation of the human and natural resources available, a detailed knowledge of the markets and sectors with potential for growth, as well as for training in modern management and marketing techniques. People in rural areas tend see themselves as the guardians of the environment and of traditional ways, and they often find it harder than city-dwellers to adjust to change... Rural areas enjoy another advantage as regards local development: social cohesion and a sense of local identity are features which become all the stronger when an area is threatened with decline. A common past and shared anxieties about the future help to create bonds and galvanise energies. Reviving long forgotten traditional crafts and local cultural or architectural heritage are very exciting activities that can rally support from rural residents, old and new. The hardest problem to overcome in rural areas often seem to be linked to a lack of fresh ideas and potential entrepreneurs, hence the need for development agencies, which must devise new ways of arousing a spirit of enterprise in villages and provide support for new activities until they are successfully established.

Source: "Local Development: New Horizons", *Innovation and Employment,* No. 3, OECD-ILE Programme, December 1989.

an example of a regional approach to rural development which involves many public and private actors.

The competitive advantage which Litschau seeks to establish in its marketing is its unspoiled natural beauty and traditional rural culture, within a larger region which stresses natural healthfulness ("The Healthiest Corner of Austria"). The approach is obviously aimed at the public's growing concern with health, the wholesome image of rural areas, and people's willingness to spend time and money to promote their well-being. As in the Amagase case, the evolving partnership of many local actors in both the public and private sectors is an advantage in building a mutually reinforcing, region-wide approach in the highly competitive tourism sector. It also produces valuable by-products in the form of community and regional solidarity.

Three major elements which have contributed to the success of the project are training schemes for local people, good marketing, and adequate public funding. From the outset, local people were involved in the activity and were professionally trained for their new roles. It was considered of great importance that managers in the holiday village and other providers of services to the public display a high level of professionalism in their work. Marketing has been vigorous, through newspapers and posters, publication of calendars of events, maps and guidebooks, and bags and T-shirts with the logo. A unified regional approach to marketing has been used. This maximises resources and quality, and concentrates on the single theme of the healthfulness of the region. Significant federal and provincial funds have been invested to support the planning process, and provide necessary infrastructure.

The project has had significant effects on the local economy. Since its outset, 55 new jobs (seasonally averaged) have been created in the village; 80 new persons have been employed in local businesses; and 350 temporary jobs have been provided. Direct revenue for Litschau and the revenue induced by tourism (payroll and beverage taxes and tourist taxes) have risen more than 60 per cent in the past seven years. These effects stemmed from differentiating services and activities, improving the quality of services (*e.g.* rooms and beds), and expanding or creating facilities for new activities such as golf, swimming, riding, biking, tennis and squash.

In contrast to other cases, this niche market strategy arose as an integral part of a regional development scheme. Marketing the holiday village to a selected group of tourists was part of a larger plan which included several related projects. Various forms of assistance, including financial and technical assistance, were provided at the appropriate stages in development. The project was managed by the local government. Private entrepreneurs were also involved in the project and in spin-off activities. Management of the project was supported by a consulting team, part of whose cost was provided by the federal government.

Chapter 3

Key Elements for Success – Provisional Conclusions

As noted at the outset, this study takes a heuristic approach. Case studies can yield useful insights, but by their nature, cannot support *definitive conclusions*. This section sets out several *provisional conclusions* in the form of the basic lessons to be drawn from the case studies for those interested in adopting or encouraging niche market businesses as part of a strategy for development in rural areas. This includes both local people and officials, and central government policy makers. From a research perspective, these lessons should be regarded as hypotheses for further, more intensive research.

A review of the case studies suggests several elements which are important in creating, developing or maintaining a niche market business. These elements are common to all of the case studies, although they differ in degree of apparent importance from one case to another. Not surprisingly, most of the same elements have analogues in general rural development strategies. The elements identified here include resource identification, inherent factors of competitive advantage, territorial linkage (in all the cases chosen for this study), advertising, information, communication and transport networks, financial and technical assistance, regulatory measures which are necessary for some niche market businesses and helpful to others, and regular re-evaluation. This section will elucidate these elements and discuss the key roles they play in developing the niche markets in the case studies.

Identification of Resources

In its 1993 publication, *What Future For Our Countryside? A Rural Development Policy,* OECD stressed the importance for rural areas of realising their comparative advantages. Many rural areas have untapped or underdeveloped resources; some are unique or at least very specific to their location. All of the case studies exemplify new uses for existing resources. The matrix used in Section 1 to categorise niche markets can be used to help identify these resources systematically and comparatively. The first step is to identify resources and assess their potential for development. Once the basic resources have been identified, a strategy to differentiate them further can be used to gain a competitive advantage in the market. The special "healthful quality" of the rural region around Litschau and the handicraft skills in Norway are typical examples. Human

39

resources, such as traditional skills or the capability for innovation or even entrepreneurship, form the basis for any development effort and are essential to the effective use of other resources.

Conclusion: The identification and assessment of resources for economic development should be a starting point for niche market strategies. Planning should be carried out with a view to the long-term prospects for realising economic potential, and the development of human resources logically ought to receive the highest priority.

Factors of Competitive Advantage

Competitive advantages stem from various factors in the process of transforming resources into goods or services for an economically viable niche markets. Key components common to all the cases, however, include local initiative, entrepreneurship, and successful partnerships.

Initiative: Local initiative plays a pivotal role in developing competitive advantages for a niche market, particularly in planning and launching the business. As an OECD study on the subject[8] describes it, *"The originality of local initiatives lies in their diversity and capacity to stimulate change on the basis of a wide range of local problems, resources and actors. Their novelty derives less from their content than from their ability to generate new procedures, patterns of behaviour and organisation."* Initiative is often synonymous with leadership. Indigenous leaders, whether private citizens or local government officials, can encourage local people to undertake challenges, guide them toward specified goals, and generate creative ideas. In the Japanese case study, for example, local government leaders persuaded farmers to switch to new products from traditional rice production.

Entrepreneurship: Entrepreneurship is used variously to describe the capacity for innovation, good management and organisational skills, or a set of attributes including initiative, creativity, willingness to risk, and sensitivity to the business environment. Unfortunately, many local population who wish to develop niche markets lack these qualities. W.E. During[9] has described the kind of behaviour that leads to business failures: *"There are no initiatives to set new goals or to execute tasks in a new way; there is little or no reaction with regard to new developments in the environment; people do not dare to get outside the given rules; the organisation has little feeling for actual problems in the field; norms and motivations are system-oriented instead of client-oriented."*

Partnership: Partnership is a collaboration among various actors such as local residents, different levels of government and private enterprise. Various partners contribute the resources, financing, management skills or training and marketing expertise necessary to develop a business and reduce risks. In the most successful cases, good partnerships strengthen business organisation, maximise the use of human and other local resources, establish information networks, and expand the market for niche goods and services. The French case study, in particular, demonstrates how local associations work well together to increase the economic potential for both niche goods and services, and the Norway Crafts provides an invaluable network of information on markets.

Conclusion: After the identification of key resources, the most important factors are initiative, entrepreneurship and partnership. They are necessary to enhance competitive advantages and further develop the markets for niche goods and services.

Organisational Structure

Most case studies indicated a specific organisational structure at the beginning of niche market development. Various types of organisation are reported: farmers' associations in the Amagase case, local producer groups in the Magnoac project and a non-profit organisation in the Elliot Lake study. Organising local people to establish businesses can produce benefits such as willingness to take risks, easy access to market information, establishment of partnerships and a more cohesive community. Moreover, through effective organisational structures, technology transfer and financial assistance become more apparent and easily attainable for niche market activities.

Conclusion: The organisational structure focuses on shared interests in developing niche market activities. They are designed to help local entrepreneurs overcome handicaps and develop their advantages, both in starting up the business and maintaining the market.

Territorial Linkage

This study selected several cases where niche goods and services are linked to territorial images, because cases where this is possible are probably more common to rural areas than cases where a rural area has an advantage in a particular industrial sector, for example. Recognising that rural entrepreneurs may also use niche goods that are not territorially linked in the minds of consumers, such as the roses of Amagase, and that not all rural areas can easily avail themselves of a territorial image, the territorial linkage is still of special interest for rural places.

One successful niche market strategy has been to promote nation-wide name recognition so that consumers will come to identify certain products with specific towns or regions. Both the Magnoac commune of France and the Waldviertel region in Austria have established for their products and services images associated with region and quality. When this approach is developed to its full potential, as in Cognac or Champagne, for example, local and regional identities do not only enhance the value of the product, but also increase economic opportunities in the service and tourism sectors in the commune or region.

Conclusion: Territorial images can have a powerful appeal to consumers. One notable and increasingly common strategy for marketing niche goods and services is to link them to such images as specific landscapes, cultural traditions or historic monuments.

Box 6. Regional identity: The complexity of identity processes

Identity in our era can no longer be based exclusively on the quest for and veneration of its roots and traditions. Such a trend would sow the seed of asphyxia. Identity thus has no sense unless it is also faced and associated with dissimilarities of the present and the future.

These ideas are valid for the regions and for all kinds of groups. It is through contacts with other regions and groups that a region builds its identity in a multitude of ways.

Even when a region does not have very specific cultural characteristics, it forges an identity which becomes a very significant factor in its development. The regional actors often use terms other than identity: image, emblem, symbol, etc. Each of these terms of course has specific content, but for simplicity's shake we will use only the term regional identity.

Regional identity is the image which the individuals and groups of one region forge in their relationship with other regions. This self-image may vary in complexity and it can be based on a past or present heritage, on a natural environment, on history, on a project for the future, on a specific economic activity, or on a combination of these various factors. While cultural identity is cultural process, it has not only cultural foundations. Furthermore, this representation is to some extent negotiated with actors outside the region.

This regional identity is often stimulating for its inhabitants; it installs pride in belonging, it is a source of regional cohesion and it encourages a desire to act for the region. Clearly, this identity is rarely accepted unanimously, since what is an emblem for some is a stigma for others. Some people often criticise regional identity on the grounds that it may cause the region to withdraw into itself, at a time when horizons are widening everywhere. It is therefore much better to encourage cosmopolitan attitudes. This debate re-emerges in very different contexts, and yet there is no incompatibility between regional identity and awareness of the world – on the contrary: greater open-mindedness means that the regional identity must be strong and shared. A region will be more of a dynamic and authentic partner of the other regions of Europe and the rest of the world if its identity is living. Nevertheless, regional identity is not a universal panacea, nor should it become so, but it is an important aspect of regional development...

Source: Culture and Regions of Europe, p. 185, Michel Bassand, Council of Europe Press, 1993.

Advertising

Advertising strategies seem to be decisive in the success of niche market businesses. All of the case studies describe well-planned advertising strategies using brochures, posters, calendars, mailings, T-shirts with logos, or other techniques. More particularly,

Litschau's Holiday Village and Magnoac use slogans which link niche goods and services to the image of area or town. This facilitates the linkage of products to territories mentioned above. Magnoac also uses direct marketing, which combines advertising with sales by mail order.

Conclusion: Advertising expands the market for niche goods, simultaneously creating an image of quality for specific products, the region, or both. Advertising is especially important for niche market goods and services produced in rural areas because rural markets are normally small and these products are by definition targeted to outside markets.

Information, Communication and Transport Networks

Several of the case studies underline the importance of an information and communication networks for rural firms in creating and marketing their niche goods and services. Norway Crafts stresses its importance for giving new impetus to traditional handicraft activities, while the Amagase case shows the importance of both an advanced transport system for developing a niche market for cut flowers in urban centres and a network to provide current information about prices and conditions in the market. Information and transport costs are often high in rural areas because of their geographical isolation. Poor communication systems often impede the development of niche market businesses even if local resources would otherwise make an enterprise economically viable.

Conclusion: Good information, communication and transport networks are important aspects of successful niche market activities. They can help to improve the quality of products, reduce costs, and avert some of the risks of changes in market demand.

Technical and Financial Assistance

The way in which cases were selected for inclusion in this study, *i.e.* through nomination by OECD governments, makes it not surprising that governments play a role in each case. This is appropriate as the study is primarily intended to help OECD governments which are interested in measures to promote rural development. Directly or indirectly, most case study authors point to the lack of technical and/or financial assistance available to rural people as major obstacles to developing niche market businesses. In these cases assistance from one or more levels of government was critical in transforming local resources into economically viable activities. In fact, various types of financial and technical assistance are available from different levels of government in most Member countries. As an unique case, the Elliot Lake case study demonstrates that tax treatment helped to promote the programme. This study neither sought nor received sufficient information to permit a detailed analysis of the nature or effectiveness of the various assistance programmes that benefited the activities in the cases reviewed. There is general agreement that for reasons of efficiency, assistance from governments should not include market distorting, long term subsidies. Most of the government assistance to the niche market businesses, as described in the case studies, was directed at providing information or reducing the costs of establishing the businesses, including initial financing. The objective was clearly to establish a self-sustaining, market-oriented economic activity.

Conclusion: Government provided technical or financial assistance can help establish economically feasible niche market projects that would otherwise probably not be possible. However, such aid should be adapted to local resources and supportive of project goals that are oriented to the market.

Regulatory Measures

The Amvrakikos case study, especially, shows the importance of environmental and land use regulations which are in harmony with a strategy for one type of niche service, eco-tourism. Because tourism in rural areas often depends on the environmental and aesthetic qualities of an area larger than any single proprietor or village can control, concerted action through regulatory measures by intermediate or central governments is sometimes necessary. More controversial, but similar in purpose, are systems to protect territorially identified products, and hence the image of a locale. It is such a local image that people are working to establish in the Magnoac case, for example.

In France, INAO (l'Institut National des Appellations d'Origine) identifies the origin and quality of agricultural products which are specific to geographic regions or produced by traditional methods. They issue AOC (Appellation d'Origine Contrôlée) labels for products after a strict approval process. Japan uses a similar system for agricultural products. In the United States a much looser form of protection is applied selectively, through laws that require "truth in labelling". In recent years the European Community has established PGI/PDO (Protected Geographical Area/Protected Designation of Origin) which provides the framework for a system of protection for agricultural products and foodstuffs eligible to carry a geographical indication or designation of origin.[10] Although such labelling alone does not create niche markets, it is a form of protection for the producer's investment in the quality or uniqueness of his products and for the identity that some rural communities are seeking to build.

The AOC approach is sometimes criticised as a device to forestall competition based on the inherent qualities of the product. To the extent it is a component of a product differentiation strategy, that is true. But the same is equally true of the protection given to manufactures for their product names, brand names, slogans, and logos by trade marks. The value of all such labelling and advertising devices depends, finally, on the consumer's judgement of their meaning.

Conclusion: Environmental and land use regulations are often necessary for the development and protection of natural rural amenities, particularly for tourism. Other types of regulatory regimes, such a certification of origin, artisanal processing and growing procedures, can facilitate rural niche market strategies.

Re-evaluations

Periodic review and re-evaluation of activities, stressed in the case study of Amagase, is valuable for two purposes: to measure progress in developing the niche market; and to appraise any changes in market demands or consumer behaviour. It is then possible to assess what further resources are necessary to improve the product or its image and to propose ways to make marketing strategies more effective. Evidence of such re-evaluation was less clear or only implicit in most of the cases reviewed.

Conclusion: Periodic re-evaluation contributes to the overall success of the niche market project as well as to maintaining a competitive advantage in the market-place.

Appendix
CASE STUDIES

1. Floriculture Using Local Energy – Japan[11]

Origin of the Activity

For decades, many rural areas in Japan have suffered from social and economic changes such as depopulation, ageing, and declining employment. These changes have had negative effects on the rural economy and society as a whole, weakening the coherence of communities, slowing structural adjustment, and causing neglect of cultural heritage and the environment.

To counteract economic and social problems, various activities, mostly led by local initiatives, have been emerging in such areas. These initiatives include: diversifying agricultural products, concentrating more on processing farm products, and paying more careful attention to the changing preferences of urban consumers in the selection and production of crops and their marketing. These activities have the potential to provide new employment and income opportunities. Value-added or service-linked products create most new economic opportunities, particularly in remote areas where too little arable land is available to allow enhanced productivity through larger scale farming.

Food preferences have been changing. Growth in expenditures for food as a share of total family income is small, increasing 4.1 per cent from 1980 to 1991. However, a careful look shows dramatic changes in people's eating patterns: consumption of cereals has decreased; that of prepared foods and meals eaten away from home has increased, by 46.5 per cent and 18.4 per cent, respectively. People increasingly prefer value-added food products, and food businesses are becoming more service-oriented. Moreover, it is expected that consumption trends will continue to increase the demand for diverse, specialised, and high quality food products.

In addition, increasing imports of agricultural products such as meats, vegetables, fish, and processed products are providing lower cost inputs for the Japanese food industry. The increase in imports has been accelerated by the appreciation of the yen since 1985.

These changes in the agro-food sector – in both demand and supply – have stimulated the diversification of domestic agriculture which is necessary to ensure that Japanese farmers remain competitive in the market. One strategy is to focus on a specific product, responding to increasing consumer demand for special features such as high quality, simplicity, and healthfulness (Figure A1.1). In any rural area, the best approach to this strategy is to identify local resources and estimate their economic value. Doing so

Figure A1.1. Changing tastes and preferences for food commodities

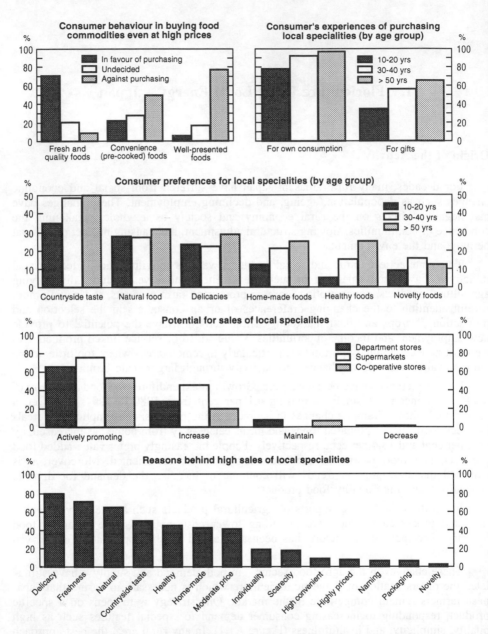

Source: Survey on Changes of Eatings Habits, Roles of Rural Area, Prime Minister's Office, 1990.

sometimes requires finding innovative ways to bring traditional skills and other local resources into play for economic development.

Many rural areas are using value-added or quality improvement strategies in agricultural products to create new markets. Oita prefecture is among these. The scheme of "Isson Ippin Undo" (One Village – One Product) originated there. In this case study the town of Amagase introduced floriculture using an unusual local resource, its hot spring.

Isson Ippin Undo

"Isson Ippin Undo" was started in 1979 by governor Hiramatsu who advocated, "Producing not *a product,* but *the product* using each town and village's own resources." Using local resources helps towns and villages establish an identity for themselves in the market. This endogenous development through community action is based on various types of local initiatives such as: building village pride, making use of competitive advantages, establishing partnerships among local people, and creating a vision of the path to development. In the past ten years, many areas have adopted this strategy to produce new products. The prefecture as a whole counts 270 new products, half of which yield annual sales above 100 million yen, including 20 products with sales exceeding one billion yen – more than 120 billion yen in total (Map A.1).

"Isson Ippin Undo" originates from the initiative, partnership and entrepreneurship of local people with little government intervention. Nevertheless, the prefectural government provides the necessary support for local people to initiate the projects. Projects include, for example:
- "Utaka no Kunizukuri Juku" (Countryside School) was established in 12 different parts of the prefecture in order for local people to exchange market information and acquire technical know-how. More than 800 people have studied in the "Juku", most of whom are now taking part actively in rural development. The Amagase case was initiated by local people who graduated from the "Juku".
- The prefecture set up a "Marketing Division" to conduct market research and advertise local products, targeting major markets in urban centres. It also gives advice to locals on designing, packaging and mailing products.
- The "Guidance Centre on Processing Agricultural and Sea Products" has conducted extensive research on products, and the new technologies and skills developed are transferred to the local people and related groups. The "Research Centre for Heating Used in Floriculture" was also established to develop floriculture projects by utilising the abundant local energy (hot spring) resources in the prefecture. The people of Amagase have a close partnership with this research centre.

Map A.1. **Products of Isson Ippin Undo in Oita prefecture**

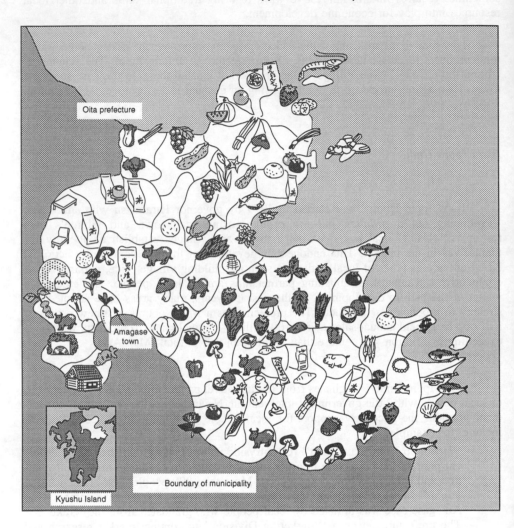

Source: Promotion group of Isson Ippin Undo in Oita prefecture.

The Area

Amagase is located in the rural western part of Oita prefecture. It is 102 km² in total area, 80 per cent of which is mountainous. It is typical of areas classified as remote. The current population is 7 900, and has been steadily declining. Those over 65 years old represent 20 per cent of the population.

The major industries are agriculture and tourism because of a local hot spring resort. Of the 3 905 people employed in Amagase, 30 per cent are in the primary sector (agriculture), 28 per cent in the secondary, and 42 per cent in the tertiary sector, of whom 46 per cent are employed in services. Based on current trends, the number of tourists is expected to grow slightly.

The agricultural sector is typical of farming in such mountainous areas. There are 1 364 total farm households, 160 consisting of professional farmers and the rest part-time farmers. The total cultivated land is 778 hectares – paddy fields 468, upland fields 126, orchards 160 and pastures 26. The average land holding is 0.57 hectares, scattered in valleys with steeply sloping land. The prevailing farming pattern is mixed, with rice, fruits, mushrooms and vegetables. However, the size of farms and geographical situation limit the potential for improving productivity. This resulted in low farm incomes and discouraged young people from taking over farms, thus accelerating out migration.

The Activity

Floriculture Using Local Energy

Urgent measures were needed to address the situation in the agricultural sector. Various strategies to diversify agricultural products and to increase income were proposed and examined among the different levels of local actors. The question of how to maximise local resources most effectively was taken into consideration. The outcome was to make Amagase the "Village with Flowers and Hot Springs". Local farmers united to create a new floriculture industry, cultivating roses by using the local hot spring as the source of energy.

Most floriculture activities use a heating system fuelled by oil which leads to high production costs. As a result, they are limited to producing a few specific varieties of flowers. Furthermore, since the oil crisis in the 1970s, the Japanese have been urged to use their own natural energy sources efficiently. Against this background, the strategy of using the local hot spring for floriculture was adopted, reducing costs as well as practising conservation. Roses were chosen after research showed that as a year-round flower, they need high temperatures to grow well. That maximised the value of using the hot spring. Production of roses is labour intensive, but there is a steady demand for them; prices are high and constant, particularly during the winter season, a time when competitors' costs are high due to their dependence on oil for heating.

Markets in urban centres were studied as were the costs of transportation. Even when the extra cost of shipping long distances is taken into account, the lower cost of the local heating system gave Amagase a competitive advantage. Because of the short shelf life of cut flowers, Amagase had an additional advantage over imported roses.

Building Partnerships

In the beginning, local government played a central role in involving farmers in the project. Time was spent explaining the outline of the plan to different groups, collecting their concerns, and working out concrete plans. Through feedback from participants and responsiveness to their concerns, mutual recognition and partnerships were built.

The major difficulty which had to be tackled was securing sufficiently large tracts of land for the floriculture facilities, namely green houses. This was a complex matter requiring a good deal of co-ordination because of the property rights of farmers whose lands were small and scattered. A co-ordinating group was established to confront the problem. Through this co-ordinating group a coherence was established, and the support of local people for the project was strengthened.

A particular effort was made to enrol young people in the project by holding a number of meetings and inviting those who had left the area for work in urban centres. The effort produced good results: 32 new entrants (25 for floriculture) were enrolled in the agricultural sector, including 18 people who had returned from urban centres (Tables A1.1 and A1.2). As no one in the area had previous experience in floriculture, new entrants needed on-the-job training in regions where floriculture was established, before the completion of the necessary facilities in Amagase.

In 1983 the first roses were shipped to the market. The flowers, however, did not sell well compared to those of competitors. Amagase flowers had low name value and recognition and lacked technical quality. Since then, thanks to many measures to improve production and marketing, the roses have succeeded well in the market, benefiting from their cost advantages, particularly in the winter season. Current statistics show that total shipments to urban centres number 3.4 million lots and total sales amount to 320 million yen annually. This has encouraged other farmers to participate in the project, producing

Table A1.1. **New entrants in the agricultural sector**

Origin of new entrants	Total	By age group				
		< 25	26-30	31-35	> 36	Average
Urban centres	18	3	2	8	5	33
Other occupations	9	0	3	3	3	34
Recently graduated	5	3	1	1	0	26
Total	32	6	6	12	8	32

Source: Amagase-town.

Table A1.2. **Farming pattern of new entrants**

	Number
Floriculture	19
Floriculture and mushroom	2
Floriculture and shiitake (mushroom)	3
Floriculture and fruits	1
Mushroom and fruits	2
Fruits	4
Livestock	1
Total	32

Source: Amagase-town.

different flowers. Floriculture producers' groups were established, and their activities have contributed to creating the image among consumers of "Amagase: A Production Centre of Flowers".

Elements of Success

Many factors were involved in producing the competitive edge which has made Amagase such a success. These are: the initiatives of local government at the outset of the project, the establishment of the producers' group to exchange information on techniques and quality improvement, market research to learn consumers' demands for species and colour, strict management and quality control in shipping lots, and steadily improving partnerships with research centres and among producer's groups.

The lower costs provided a competitive advantage in the market. This greatly depended on the efficient use of local energy. In addition, the participation of women, whose labour had not been needed in local agriculture in the past, also contributed to reducing costs. Moreover, their sense of consumer preference and the ability to make subtle distinctions in colour and smell, helped differentiate the products. All these contributing factors were supported by the entrepreneurship of the participants of the project.

Effects on the Rural Economy

Creation of Income and Employment Opportunities

The effect of the floriculture project on household incomes was significant: before the project, when the farming pattern was a combination of rice and other crops such as vegetables and fruits, the annual average farm income of full-time farmers was only 0.8 million yen. After incorporating floriculture in local farming, it increased to 2.3 million yen. Full-time floriculture farmers benefited in particular, with average incomes above 6 million yen.

The project so far has resulted in 25 new entrants into floriculture and employment for 25 women. Some of the women later became independent producers, benefiting from their experiences as employees.

Revitalisation of Agriculture and Rural Areas

Agriculture, which requires heavy work for low returns, has a poor image in the countryside. With this project, the image has changed. Local people, especially the young and women, were encouraged to diversify their income sources through floriculture. At present, all new entrants in floriculture are full-time producers and have been undertaking various related activities organised around each producers' group. This has encouraged other farmers to diversify their crops and has helped increase the number of farm households with young successors waiting to take over: from 116 households before, to 251 households after the project. They have a 50 per cent share of total agricultural production in the area.

The project also helped to improve the structure of local agriculture, from one of rice producers clinging to small plots to floriculturists using naturally heated green houses. Productivity was enhanced and farming diversified. This experience also established a model of an improved farming pattern in a mountainous area less favourable for agriculture. For Amagase Noukyo (*i.e.* the agricultural co-operative), total sales of agricultural products have increased 45 per cent in value in the past 10 years (Figure A1.2).

Many of the activities related to changing to the production of flowers have helped to activate the community and strengthen its social fabric. Floriculture producers' groups always distribute flower seedlings to people who visit the area. Customs such as planting flowers everywhere in the village have helped to promote Amagase's image as "A Village with Flowers and Hot Springs".

Overcoming Constraints

Floriculture is capital intensive; it requires investment, in particular for facilities such as green houses, which are expensive. Lack of capital often impedes otherwise willing new entrants to the project. Even when aspiring new floriculturists are able to find a lender, they often lack sufficient assets to secure a loan with a mortgage. To tackle this problem the local government, in association with Noukyo, is studying the feasibility of setting up a separate "third sector" to construct the necessary facilities and lease them to farmers who want to start floriculture operations. If this is done, the initial burden on new entrants will be reduced to some extent, allowing more people to participate in floriculture activities.

The National Chamber of Agriculture sent a questionnaire to people in 117 rural or regional basic industries asking them to list the kinds of assistance they felt they needed

Figure A1.2. **Food product sales in Amagase co-operative**

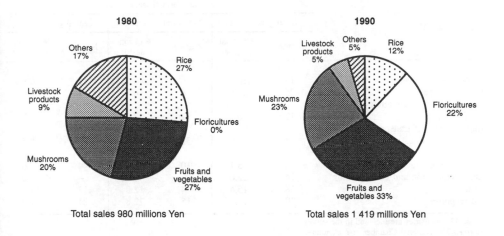

1980

Others 17%

Rice 27%

Livestock products 9%

Floricultures 0%

Mushrooms 20%

Fruits and vegetables 27%

Total sales 980 millions Yen

1990

Livestock products 5%

Others 5%

Rice 12%

Mushrooms 23%

Floricultures 22%

Fruits and vegetables 33%

Total sales 1 419 millions Yen

Source: Amagase-town.

from government (Table A1.3). The following briefly summarises the needs they expressed:

- to the local government, their priorities were for policies to secure a "successor to the businesses" (25 per cent); "land acquisition and consolidation" measures (12 per cent); and to help with "innovation and adaptation of technology" (10 per cent);
- to the prefectural government, their priorities were for help with "innovation and adaptation of technology" (27 per cent); and "improvement of transportation and communications systems" (27 per cent);
- to the central government, their first priority was for a "loan system with long terms and low interest" (38 per cent); followed by "improvement of transportation and communications systems" (19 per cent).

In the case of Amagase, various measures were taken to meet the needs mentioned above. To help secure successors, the *local government* made various efforts to recruit new entrants to floriculture, not only locally but also attracting those who had left the areas to work in urban centres. Training and skill improvement programmes were provided for new entrants, in co-operation with established producers from other areas. Setting up the association of land owners was the first step in successfully reorganising scattered plots of land to create enough space for new facilities. Help with marketing strategies focused on monitoring consumer needs and trends, providing the incentive to

Table A1.3. **Industries' requests for assistance to different levels of government**

| Type of request | Request for assistance from: | | | | | |
| | Local government | | Prefectural government | | Central government | |
	Number	% of total industries	Number	% of total industries	Number	% of total industries
Market development	19	16.2	6	5.1	1	0.9
Finding successors	25	21.4	8	6.8	3	2.6
Innovation and adaptation of technology	12	10.3	32	27.4	9	7.7
Improvement of transportation and communications systems	3	2.6	32	27.4	22	18.8
Loan programs with longterm and low interest rates	6	5.1	10	8.5	44	37.6
Land acquisition and consolidation	14	12.0	–	0.0	–	0.0
Others	18	15.4	14	12.0	17	14.5
No response	20	17.1	15	12.8	21	17.9

Note: 117 industries are included in the survey.
Source: The National Chamber of Agriculture.

differentiate products, and controlling and managing supply to keep the market constant. The *prefectural government* established research centres to provide technical support and guidance for producers. Finally, the *central government* provided agricultural structural funds for farmers to build the necessary facilities. The co-ordinated partnerships among different levels of government helped farmers overcome the difficulties they faced at the beginning of the project.

Assessment

This case shows how floriculture, using a local energy source, created a niche market through a cost advantage, and how that activity diversified income sources and employment opportunities for local farmers. The result was a shift from traditional, low productivity rice farming to more efficient capital-and labour-intensive floriculture production. This has contributed greatly to structural adjustment in the agricultural sector of the area. The same adjustment has also created jobs for women and brought about a U-turn in migration; young people are now returning from urban centres. In addition, intangible effects should not be overlooked. Among which is the revitalisation of the community through new partnerships and better management of rural resources.

This case also shows that the policies and implementing measures provided by the government encouraged local initiatives and fostered entrepreneurship among farmers as well as others in the private sector.

In a sense, the "Isson Ippin Undo" philosophy gave birth to the Amagase project and propelled it forward, even though it is not specifically a niche market strategy. Success is never guaranteed; there are always risks of failure if planning is careless, especially if the products are not chosen carefully. Furthermore, success depends on paying attention to ever changing demands and trends in the market.

2. Traditional Handicrafts – Norway[12]

The Activity

The potential in Norway for traditional handicrafts, made by a local workforce, is considerable. A growing interest in the cultural and historical attributes of rural areas is being observed among both local inhabitants and tourists.

Handicrafts have many evident advantages – they have a wide spectrum of production possibilities, from part-time independent piece-work to full-time work on an industrial scale. They are characterised by a relatively low requirement for capital, environmentally friendly production and an effective use of local resources. Production is usually locally situated and could form the basis for a decentralisation policy. They also employ a high proportion of women and contribute to the conservation of Norwegian heritage and culture.

The Area

Traditional crafts are made throughout Norway (Map A.2), in three types of sparsely populated areas. These are areas *i)* where farming plays an important economic role; *ii)* those that depend more on state provided public services for economic well-being; *iii)* and which are populated predominantly by Lappish people.

The first category consists of farming areas, especially in the mountains where the farms are small and incapable of generating sufficient income to support a whole family. There are usually difficulties in finding off-farm employment. The craft producers usually have some connection with the land: either they are farmers, or their spouses or their parents are. They may be assisted by funds administered by the Ministry of Agriculture.

The second category pertains to any area which is sparsely populated. Small enterprises are often situated there but agriculture and fisheries are often still important. Craft producers in these areas have no connection with agriculture; their products reflect local culture and often revive old traditions under a new guise.

The third category are those areas where the Sami/Lappish handicraft "duodji" is produced.[13] Production is mainly located in the north of Norway but can also be found among the Lappish people in the central and southern of Norway. These areas are again

Map A.2. **Area locations in Norway**

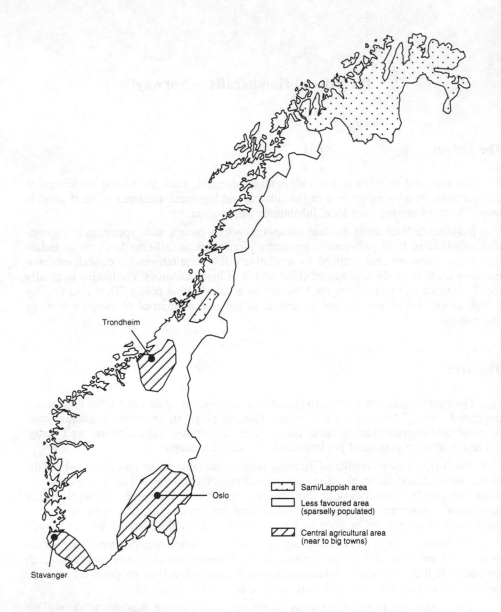

Trondheim

Oslo

Stavanger

☐ Sami/Lappish area

☐ Less favoured area
(sparselly populated)

▨ Central agricultural area
(near to big towns)

Source: Ministry of Agriculture, Norway.

sparsely populated with a high preponderance of agricultural production and reindeer herds, and little other industry. Duodji represents a long-lasting and important cultural heritage.

Duodji production is unique. It is characterised by the Sami population with their expertise in reindeer herding and strong cultural heritage, their distinctive language and ethnic background, and also by the great unpopulated mountain ranges, and far from public services, shops and town centres.

It is important for traditional handicrafts to have some connection with the local cultural heritage and traditions and the inspiration that these generate. The local areas provide the necessary base of raw materials, knowledge, expertise and sense of identity.

Origin of the Activity

More often than not these niche market activities originate with the producers themselves out of a need for additional income or of a wish to use their own skills, ideas and abilities to preserve the natural heritage and old, local traditions in handicrafts. By establishing their own businesses, producers make an important contribution to the rural development process. Moreover, these activities enable women to make use of their skills and local folklore and thus make a profitable living in rural areas which offer few stimulating employment possibilities for women.

Niche markets can also be developed by the different funding bodies and advisory services. Politicians are now concentrating on small businesses and are implementing programmes and projects in their favour. In 1990, the Ministries of Local Government and Agriculture established a private trust, entitled "Norway Crafts", responsible for project feasibility and for providing employment in this relatively ignored sector of handicrafts and traditional products. Until the end of 1994, Norway Crafts is to receive financial support totalling Nkr 30 million, Nkr 6 million each year for five years, during which period it will endeavour to become self-supporting. The project has a head office in Oslo and four regional offices in rural areas where the sale and marketing of niche goods and services is known to be difficult.

Norway Crafts is mandated to provide employment opportunities in the sectors of handicrafts and small-scale industries throughout the country, in both the Norwegian and the Lappish areas. The potential for growth is good; the aim is to create 2 000 new posts by the year 2000.

The main functions of Norway Crafts are:
- creation of a data base on handicraft activities, its market, co-operation networks, product design, product development, raw materials, production processes and distribution chains in the handicraft sector;
- dissemination of information through in-house courses, conferences, seminars and by mobilising the various advisory services;
- promotion of i) joint ventures for handicraft activities at national and international trade fairs; ii) export schemes; and iii) quality labels such as trademarks;

- establishment of privately-owned sales outlets to encourage trade, such as export companies and shops;
- improvement in the support framework for producers and assistance in developing trade.

Measures to Sustain a Niche Market

Norway Crafts, in addition to carrying out their ascribed functions, set high quality standards for producers who are affiliated with the Programme. Non-affiliated producers also receive assistance with the diverse aspects of distribution and marketing and in particular with quality, originality and the strong traditional association.

In Norway, measures taken to sustain a niche market are targeted in general to the rural areas, unless there is a specific sector, product or activity which is the subject of its own programme, project or even strategy.

Elements for Success

Important elements for the success of handicrafts are a good marketing strategy and a good network. These small-scale producers need either a channel or a network through which they are able to co-ordinate their distribution, marketing, sales and development. Of equal importance is the correct surroundings and environment for their activity. Formal and informal networks are sources of social interaction, exchange of ideas, inspiration and problem-solving.

Financial support is possibly another element for success but is of less importance if the production process is going well.

An interest in handicrafts, along with buying capability is the best environment for this type of activity. A producer, however, needs to have a sensible approach to growth and expenditure. The objective for most of these small-scale producers is not to grow large but to use their own resources, time and ideas to provide an income for themselves. The activity might include a few employees but the goal is not necessarily to expand, only to be creative and independent.

Constraints on Development

Factors which limit the success of the activity are the reverse of those just described, *i.e.* isolated production units with no access to good marketing and distribution channels.

To overcome these constraints, there is a need for the implementation of projects, programmes, training courses and networks. Ministries could be encouraged to allocate funds to provide advisory services on marketing and on improving the producers' own skills.

Effects of the Activity on Rural Areas

Employment in traditional handicrafts helps to maintain the population structure and also furthers the development of services which secure, for the rural population, a standard of living comparable with the rest of the country. The effects of handicraft activities are difficult to quantify as few studies and statistics exist to date.

The political objectives have only partly been achieved. Initiatives for rural development have been targeted at promoting entrepreneurial skills and the realisation of women's potential and ambitions. These initiatives entail changes in attitudes which take time and as yet, entrepreneurship is still in its infancy. Patience is necessary but progress, although small, is in the right direction.

Assessment

All sectors contribute to rural development and all have programmes and projects similar to Norway Crafts, as in agro-tourism, for example. Handicrafts are of interest to tourists and their dependency on a broad spectrum of other activities is noted. At Nordkapp, a tourist site, the sale of duodji is associated with the local area. Producers find there a ready-made market that they would have no possibility of reaching "alone".

A rural development strategy should target the whole country and all sectors of activity; they are inter-dependent – services and products, people and the landscape/ cultural heritage, agriculture and other industries. In future, the objective must be to find a way in which the different sectors can co-operate with one another and in which rural areas can be developed as a whole.

The role for policy is clear. A strong decentralised public service with a high level of competence in rural development and in entrepreneurship is recommended. This is important for the population and for sustaining the growth of a socio-economic and socio-cultural sector. An advisory service should also be established to promote the role of women and to protect working conditions for both men and women. Its aim is to ensure that the diverse sectors, such as agriculture, local government, and finance co-operate to enhance the rural areas, with the entrepreneur playing a central role.

3. Retirement Living in Elliot Lake – Canada[14]

Niche Market Activity

Elliot Lake's Retirement living concept is an example of niche market activity, and provides the basis for this case study. Retirement Living is a community based economic development initiative seeking to restore economic vitality to Elliot Lake by promoting the area as an ideal retirement location. The availability of quality, affordable housing, coupled with the natural amenities which surround Elliot Lake, make it an attractive choice of relocation for retirees with a disposable income who are seeking an improved quality of life. While Elliot Lake's plan mainly targets those fifty-five and over, it is not restricted to that age group.

The Area

Location

Elliot Lake is located 600 kilometres (375 miles) north of Toronto, in northern Ontario as shown on Map A.3, and has earned an enviable reputation as the "Jewel in the Wilderness". The community was originally established because of the discovery of and subsequent demand for uranium in 1953. The uranium industry boomed and Elliot Lake grew rapidly to a peak population of approximately 18 000 by 1986. The city is located 18 miles north of the Trans Canada Highway, midway between Sudbury and Sault Ste. Marie, and is part of the scenic road known as the Deer Trail, a 120 mile route through northern Ontario which extends through Mississagi Provincial Park and encompasses numerous lakes and streams. The community is surrounded by natural beauty; a hilly terrain with an abundance of trees and fresh air.

Difference of the Rural Area as Compared to Others

Although other rural areas in northern Ontario boast of natural amenities as attractive as those of Elliot Lake, no other community can match the available, affordable, retirement housing which Elliot Lake suddenly had to offer. This excess housing, result-

Source: OECD Secretariat.

ing from mine closures and downsizing, combined with affordability, natural amenities and a solid infrastructure, placed Elliot Lake in a unique position to take full advantage of the opportunity to develop a successful retirement community.

Origin of the Activity

Elliot Lake has suffered huge swings in population since its establishment in 1953 because of the boom and bust cycle inherent in being a single industry town and displacement in the demand for its product. Figure A3.1 illustrates the drastic change in the population in the thirty-five year history of Elliot Lake. In the early 1960s the uranium boom brought miners and their families to the community. By the mid-sixties a sharp decline in the demand for uranium forced many residents to leave Elliot Lake. However, due to protests against the industry closing, the Canadian government started stockpiling uranium and the industry that kept Elliot Lake populated began to boom again in the mid-seventies. By the late eighties the mines once again became threatened and by the dawn of the nineties the uranium industry had been declared redundant in Elliot Lake. If history was to repeat itself, the community would soon drop in population like it did in the late sixties with the closing of the mines. However, because of the Retirement Living concept the population has declined only a fraction, though the total population has continued to decline slightly throughout the early 1990s. To date the influx of retirees to the area has somewhat compensated for the outmigration of much of the younger working-age population.

With a thriving uranium industry Elliot Lake was expected to become a city of 30 000 residents. By the early 1980s a new townsite was completed, offering an abundance of attractive housing units for miners and their families. Elliot Lake spent millions of dollars developing an adequate infrastructure for the population which would be drawn to the community to participate in the mining industry. Improvements such as sewage and water treatments plants, pumping stations, forcemains and related works were constructed as well as a six million dollar expansion to the local hospital. But, by the end of the

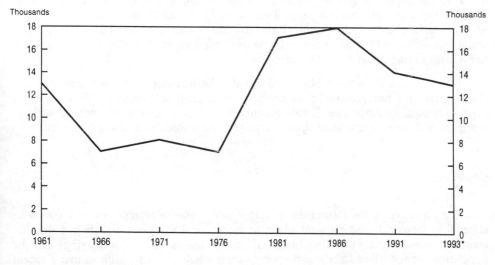

Figure A3.1. **Population of Elliot Lake**

* Data for 1993 are estimated.
Source: Statistics Canada.

69

decade Elliot Lake's uranium ore body was sorely depleted and of considerably lower grade than elsewhere in Canada. Rio Algom Ltd. has operated three uranium mines in Elliot Lake: the Quirke, Panel and Stanleigh mines. The Quirke and Panel mines closed in August 1990, terminating some 1 700 employees. Denison Mines operated one mine in Elliot Lake. In 1991, Denison Mines announced that Ontario Hydro had given Notice of Termination of its uranium supply contract, effective January 1, 1993 and that it would close its operation permanently upon completion of contract deliveries, affecting some 1 000 workers. Approximately 3 000 residents have become or will become unemployed. The full impact of the mine closure on the community will not be felt until 1996, when the final contract between Ontario Hydro and Rio Algom Ltd. comes to an end.

With this decline in mining in Elliot Lake, it became apparent that there was a surplus of rental housing and no tenants, since many of the miners had left the community. The maintenance of the housing units soon became a costly liability for the mine owners. Having seen the success of planned retirement communities in places such as Florida (USA) and recognising that the demographics of Canada indicated that seniors would make up a growing segment of the population in future years, the Deputy Mayor who was also the Vice-President of Denison Mines in charge of Community Relations and Housing, decided that the Retirement Living concept could be applied to Elliot Lake. If people with a disposable income who did not require employment could be encouraged to move to Elliot Lake and occupy the empty housing units, the cost of maintaining the vacant rental units, could be dramatically alleviated.

Although not initially a major success, the evidence of interest in Elliot Lake as a retirement community resulted in the establishment of the Non Profit Senior Housing of Elliot Lake Corporation to manage the retirement community concept promotion. In 1987, the Deputy Mayor approached the two mining companies and asked each to contribute to a promotional campaign. Both Rio Algom and Denison Mines contributed $25 000 each. The Municipality of Elliot Lake also contributed $25 000 to the promotional activities. With this combined financial support of $75 000 the Elliot Lake Retirement Living campaign was underway.

Rio Algom and Denison Mines "donated" the housing to the Non Profit Senior Housing and in return received a tax credit for their charitable donation. This became a huge advantage for Retirement Living because they owned the property outright with no mortgage and no debt and were thus able to provide affordable housing to retirees.

Objectives

The objective of the Retirement Living concept was to promote Elliot Lake as an affordable, beautiful, and pleasant place to retire. In doing so it was hoped that the economy would cease to decline (many of the mining families were leaving) and the population base of Elliot Lake and property values would stabilise (with so many vacant lots, property values were drastically declining and thus, were becoming extremely affordable).

Policies for Niche Market

The Retirement Living concept was a locally based initiative. Several programs and policies were initiated to promote Elliot Lake as a retirement community. For example, the Parks and Recreation Department has developed more seniors-oriented programs and City Council has passed a by-law which ensures that seniors with low incomes who qualify to receive a supplementary income to their Canadian Pension Plan and Old Age Security are given a $150 tax break if they own property in Elliot Lake. The entire community has attempted to involve retirees in the community. Businesses that cater to retirees needs tend to do better financially than those that do not. The undeclared policy for integration and acceptance into the Elliot Lake community seems to be a main means of developing the concept of Retirement Living.

Measures to Sustain the Market

In 1993, the population of Elliot Lake was approximately 13 500. Of that population there are currently 1 500 seniors, most of whom have migrated to Elliot Lake for retirement. Many of these retirees rent their accommodation from Retirement Living, some have purchased their own homes. Several steps have been taken to sustain the Retirement Living idea. First, and most important, are the advertising campaigns that have been run throughout Ontario promoting Elliot Lake as a perfect place to retire. Newspapers, magazines, television, promotional videos, radio and brochures have all been incorporated into the Retirement Living campaign. Perhaps the most valuable promotion of all has been the Retirement Living caravans that travel throughout Ontario. The caravan transports seniors from Elliot Lake around the province where they talk to potential renters. If someone is interested in Elliot Lake they are sent brochures and pamphlets of the Retirement Living concept which include retirement accommodation and details of the services and recreational facilities. Prospective clients are invited to visit the community and are treated to two free nights accommodation and a guided tour of the city and available real estate.

The Retirement Living market is sustained by maintaining the lowest possible cost for rental accommodation. Without affordable quality housing units there would be no viable market

Finally, while affordable housing is the initial attraction to Elliot Lake, to continue to entice more people to relocate to the community there is a need to provide activities to sustain a retirement community.

Elements of Success

There are many reasons why Elliot Lake has been successful to-date as a retirement community. Primary, of course, is the wide selection of housing options available at

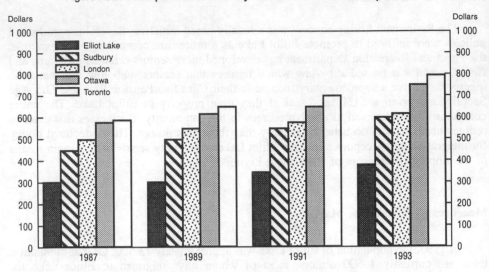

Figure A3.2. **Comparison of monthly rent for a two bedroom apartment**

Source: Canada Mortgage and Housing Corp.

extremely competitive prices. As Figure A3.2 illustrates, the cost of accommodation for a two bedroom apartment in Elliot Lake is significantly lower than in other centres south of Elliot Lake.

This lower cost of housing promotes a higher quality of life in many respects. With less expensive housing retirees are left with more disposable income. In many cases this leaves the retired citizens with extra money to enjoy activities such as travel that they may otherwise not be able to afford.

Yet there are other reasons that attract retirees to Elliot Lake. People come because they want to escape the fast-paced life-style of larger communities. Elliot Lake offers a slow, more relaxed environment with an infrastructure that caters to the needs of its seniors and retired residents. Due to the smallness of the community, seniors are attracted to the possibility that they may be able to impact the way in which their community operates.

Two related elements that contribute to the success of Elliot Lake as a retirement community are the natural beauty and healthy environment. Many claim that the air is cleaner and the trees, lakes and picturesque scenery add to the attraction and hence to the success of Elliot Lake. The natural environment is conducive to both active and passive outdoor activities encouraging activities such as hiking and nature walks, picnicking, birdwatching, and skiing. Elliot Lake is surrounded with many lakes which provide year-round fishing, boating and swimming, and, in the winter months, snowmobiling.

72

Elliot Lake, as a retirement community provides many active retirees with a myriad of recreational options.

The relatively small population and size of Elliot Lake provide the opportunity for community members to get to know each other. This friendly nature of the community provides a strong sense of belonging and safety, both important issues to retirees.

Paramount to the success of Elliot Lake and the promotion of the area as a viable retirement community is the commitment and innovative thinking by leaders on behalf of community members. Elliot Lake, like many other single industry towns, could have quietly folded and become just another vacant mining town. Yet the members of the Elliot Lake business community wanted to see Elliot Lake survive despite its economic hardships. Their perseverance and dedication played a vital role in the initial success of the Retirement Living concept. Continued efforts in marketing and market research are other factors that contribute to the success of this endeavour. Included in this notion of community commitment is the co-operation from the mining companies in playing an active and helpful role in the Retirement Living concept.

Public funding has also been a key to the success of Elliot Lake. Over $10 million was contributed by the federal government for training and other programs. The Ontario Government undertook a number of initiatives that had a direct impact on the Retirement Living program. In December 1990, $15 million was provided to assist with economic diversification and revitalisation of Elliot Lake and surrounding areas. Of the $15 million, $7 million was allocated to the Retirement Living program. Some of those funds were used to renovate many of the mining houses, making them suitable for retirement accommodation.

In June 1991, the Government of Ontario announced a $250 million package to help Elliot Lake and the surrounding communities make the transition from a dependence on uranium mining to a more diversified economy. There are three elements to this, all of which were to be delivered by Ontario Hydro. These included $65 million to help area communities adjust in the short term and diversify their economic base in the long term; $25 million for a number of energy initiatives, such as local energy efficiency programs and a commitment to purchase from Rio Algom's Stanleigh mine until 1996.

Constraints on Development

Factors Potentially Limiting Success

There are several factors that could potentially limit the success of the Retirement Living program in Elliot Lake. The first is the geography of the area. The terrain of the city and the surrounding area consists mostly of hills and rock outcroppings which, while beautiful, can make accessibility difficult for seniors/retirees. Severe winter weather conditions also pose a challenge to the program and could limit the market to those retirees who can afford to winter in a more southernly climate. The combination of difficult terrain and bitter winters restricts the potential market of Retirement Living to active and physically fit seniors/retirees.

Elliot Lake's location in a relatively remote part of Ontario, compared to larger population concentrations, also represents a limit to its success as most individuals eventually retire within a 100 kilometres radius of their original hometown or family. This could mean that only those seniors/retirees who once lived in Elliot Lake or the surrounding area would commit to remaining for a substantial period. Retirees who are attracted from areas outside of northern Ontario may only view Elliot Lake as temporary change in location which ultimately could result in a transitory senior/retiree population.

Another factor limiting the success of Retirement Living is the lack of social and health facilities that are geared towards ageing in place (long-term care). Currently there are facilities for independent living and for 24-hour ambulatory care but no facility to cover the range of needs that falls between these two extremes. In addition, there is limited availability for in-home services for the aged. This situation is compounded by the community's dependence on federal and provincial government funding for the provision of these services.

Ironically, the success that Retirement Living has experienced in attracting seniors based on the notion of affordability has the potential to limit the amount of economic benefit that may be derived. Those who choose to move to Elliot Lake to stretch their pension dollars tend to be extremely conscious of the amount of money they spend.

Discontinuation of community support for the Retirement Living program could limit success or result in the demise of the program altogether. This entails adapting to the presence of an older population in a town that is used to being middle-aged and younger. Businesses and services that do not alter their operations to accommodate the needs of seniors/retirees may eventually contribute to their decision to return to their previous area of residence.

Finally, Elliot Lake suffers from negative images in the popular media and in the minds of the general public due to its relationship with the uranium industry. Elliot Lake's proximity to radiation sources contributes to the fear of related health risks. Although the relationship between increased health problems and closeness to uranium mines has not been conclusively proven, this has the potential to limit the success of Retirement Living.

Measures to Overcome Constraints

One measure that is currently being employed to overcome some of the aforementioned constraints involves an ongoing marketing and advertising program. The aim is the keep the occupancy levels of Retirement Living's housing units at 90 per cent of capacity by continually attracting new seniors/retirees to the area. Overcoming the negative image of a mining town, especially one involving uranium, is another objective of this marketing effort.

The second major measure that is being used to reduce the limitations to success is the integration of seniors/retirees into the community in as many ways as possible. This requires community recognition of the issues that are facing the senior/retiree population and the establishment of more services to meet their particular needs. Some training sessions for local retailers have been organised by Retirement Living to sensitise salespeople to the requirements of an older clientele. While adjusting to the needs of seniors/ retirees, it has been recognised that singling them out from the general populace by offering seniors' discounts can be counter-productive to the goal of integrating them into the community.

Effects of Activity

Since the beginning of the Retirement Living program, over 3 000 seniors/retirees have moved to Elliot Lake at one point or another. Ninety-seven per cent of the retirees have come from the province of Ontario. The senior citizen population (age 65 and older) increased from 2.64 per cent in 1986 to 8.49 per cent in 1991. The percentage of the population aged 55 to 64 has also increased from 4.98 to 9.12 per cent, representing an influx of individuals who are taking advantage of early retirement. Figure A3.3 illustrates the dramatic increases in the older age groups of the population of Elliot Lake.

The seniors/retirees who have moved to Elliot Lake occupied 1 145 of Retirement Livings' 1 600 available housing units as of November 1993, a figure that accounts for approximately 20 per cent of the total number of occupied private dwellings. This makes Retirement Living the largest single land owner and tax payer within the city.

Figure A3.3. **Percentage change by age group, Elliot Lake 1986-1991**

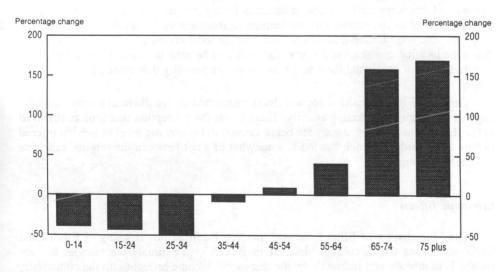

Source: Statistics Canada 1986, 1991.

75

Social Effects

Probably the most significant and positive social impact is the sense of hope that the Retirement Living program has brought to the community. The program is the first large-scale success that the community has experienced in its efforts to diversify the local economy.

However, the success of Retirement Living can be a double-edged sword in that it could also contribute to false expectations on the part of the community. There is a danger that the community could view Retirement Living as its salvation and subsequently relax its efforts to become economically diverse. The future of Elliot Lake is unlikely to be sustained solely on the Retirement Living Concept, other economic developments are also needed.

A second impact revolves around the human resources of the community. The influx of retirees into Elliot Lake has increased the pool of skills within the community as each retiree brings with them a lifetime of skills and experiences.

The new residents thus far exhibit a high degree of volunteerism and are active participants in the community, making Elliot Lake a better place for all.

It would seem that Elliot Lake has undergone a dramatic change in outlook with respect to the value of the community as a whole, partially as a result of the Retirement Living program. There appears to have been a shift away from a transitory, "frontier town" mentality to one that is more rooted in a sense of heritage. The retirees have chosen to come to Elliot Lake for reasons beyond the employment possibilities that attracted people for the first thirty years of Elliot Lake's brief history.

The Retirement Living program also had an impact on the services that are offered in the community. As new arrivals, the retirees inquire into the programs available or lacking and this serves to focus added attention on these same services. The program has also contributed to the community by helping to maintain such services as schools and hospitals. The contribution that retirees make to the local tax base and their participation in adult education courses has become significant in helping to support the local school boards. Levels of provincial funding for hospitals are partially determined by the level of usage.

Despite all of the positive social effects mentioned above, there are some negative impacts of the niche marketing activity. There exists the perception that seniors involved in the Retirement Living program are being catered to beyond the level of service offered to long-time residents which has led to somewhat of a rift between the original residents and the new-comers.

Economic Effects

The Municipality of Elliot Lake and the Non Profit Senior Housing of Elliot Lake Corporation uses the calculation detailed in Box A3. to estimate the number of jobs created both directly and indirectly by the disposable income brought into the community by the retirees.

```
┌─────────────────────────────────────────────────────────────────────────┐
│                                                                           │
│                Box A3.  Estimation of job creation                        │
│                                                                           │
│   • Average annual income retiree brings to Elliot Lake = $15 000.        │
│   • Average number of occupants in a Retirement Living housing unit = 1.7.│
│   • Total number of Retirement Living housing units = 1 600.              │
│   • Average occupancy rate = 75% total number of units = 1 200.           │
│     (average income)/(average number of occupants)/                       │
│     (average occupancy) = $30 600 000.                                    │
│                                                                           │
│   Assume:    every $40 000 brought into the community is the equivalent   │
│              of one full-time job.                                        │
│                                                                           │
│   Therefore: 765 direct and indirect jobs are created.                    │
│                                                                           │
│   ─────────                                                               │
│                                                                           │
│   Source: Municipality of Elliot Lake and Non Profit Senior Housing of    │
│   Elliot Lake Corporation.                                                │
│                                                                           │
└─────────────────────────────────────────────────────────────────────────┘
```

In addition to the direct and indirect jobs that have been created by the Retirement Living program, a number of jobs were preserved by the influx of the disposable income of the retirees. The number of layoffs that were prevented in the local service industry is difficult to assess. As noted earlier, the retirees help maintain many jobs in the health and medical professions in the community and a similar occurrence can be expected at local services such as banks and financial institutions. Since 1991, 67 new businesses have opened in Elliot Lake, with 57 of them still in operation at the end of 1993. On the down side, however, 39 businesses which had opened before 1991 were closed by the end of 1993. This leaves Elliot Lake with a net gain of 18 businesses. Most of the business closures during this period are attributable to the continued downsizing of the mining operations. There is a shift in the type of new businesses resulting from the success of the Retirement Living program. Among the businesses that were created between 1991 and 1993, and still operating, eight offer in-home and home maintenance services (*e.g.* security systems, handiwork, janitorial services), four are beauty salons or hairdressers, six deal in craft/hobby supplies or books, and three are eating establishments.

The disposable income which the retirees bring to Elliot Lake is estimated to be 30 million dollars per annum.

An important point to note about the Retirement Living program is the manner in which the economic impacts of the activity differ from those of a traditional source of employment such as the mines. The Retirement Living program does not purchase from the local area the same amount of supplies, equipment or materials that the mines once did. Additionally, instead of two sources of municipal tax revenue (property of employees and property of the mines) the Retirement Living program establishes one source in its role of landlord.

The Retirement Living program has created a spin-off industry in the form of increased tourism due to family visits. During the summer the retirees attract their immediate and extended families to the area. They come to enjoy the outdoors and take full advantage of the available hiking trails, fishing and local beaches. This influx of visitors to the community increases hotel occupancy and spending at local gift shops, stores, restaurants and the other services of Elliot Lake.

Achievement of Objectives

For the most part, the original policy objectives of Retirement Living, the Municipality of Elliot Lake and the two mining companies have been largely met: a high percentage of the houses have been filled; population loss has been slowed down; the community has maintained its viability; and the local tax base has been preserved. However, there is a need for ongoing efforts towards the fulfilment of long-term goals such as the establishment of a facility that offers one window health and social services for the retirees. In addition, Retirement Living has encountered some difficulty meeting their projection of 90 per cent occupancy in its housing units and if this level is to be achieved and maintained it will require continuous marketing efforts.

Assessment of Niche Market Activity

Usefulness for Other Rural Areas

A program like Retirement Living has potential as one component of a development strategy for other rural areas. However, it should be kept in mind that the Elliot Lake case was the product of a unique set of circumstances. There was an uncommon overabundance of affordable housing stock that would be difficult to find elsewhere. This housing was owned by only two entities as opposed to a multitude of private owners and this eased the process of consolidating the housing stock. The process through which Retirement Living was developed was also unique in that there were very strong ties between the mining companies and the municipal government. However, a vital element in the success of Elliot Lake is the availability of natural resources for recreational purposes.

Despite the uniqueness of the Elliot Lake case, there is potential for the development of smaller scale Retirement Living programs in other rural communities, especially other single industry or resource towns, which are located in areas of natural beauty. Though the relative simplicity of a Retirement Living Project appears constrained only by the amount of housing that would be available, the provision of an adequate supporting infrastructure, including medical care facilities and other social services, is an important factor to be considered.

Rural communities have a lot to offer retirees on fixed incomes who desire the highest possible quality of life that their financial situation can support. Retirement Living addresses the desires of an increasingly ageing population and provides a location where retirees can feel more financially, physically, and psychologically secure.

Role for Policy

There is a definite role for policy in activities such as Retirement Living. Generally speaking, policy is required to set the goals and objectives of the program in such a manner as to ensure an holistic approach. There is a need for policy to focus attention on long-term goals. In terms of government policies (federal/provincial/municipal) there is a need for support and financial assistance. Encouragement of private investment, support/ approval of development proposals, and capital and infrastructure expenditures are other areas where government policy can have a role in this type of program.

4. Ecological Tourism in the Amvrakikos Gulf – Greece[15]

The Activity

The Amvrakikos Gulf planning area comprises a vast wetland complex including a double river delta, three large and several small lagoons, lakes and marshes. This complex is the habitat or resting place of rare and endangered bird species, protected by international conventions and EC directives. The same wetlands are traditional fishing grounds and are also used for lagoon culture. It is a beautiful, relatively well-preserved area, with many unusual features.

KEPE, the Government Centre for Planning and Economic Research, devised the Amvrakikos Programme in the belief that these features could be the basis of a particular form of "mild" tourism, adapted to the unusual natural environment and its associated activities and compatible with its preservation. "Eco-tourism" would be only one of a set of minor tourist activities, that would also include agro-tourism, cultural and scientific tourism and water sports, to complement the more general holiday tourism centred mainly on the beaches of the Ionian coast, but also on those of the Gulf itself. These alternative forms of tourism would enhance the other features of the area and attract income to the rural hinterland.

Eco-tourism, based on the birds and other distinguishing features of the wetlands, is a relatively new idea in Greece compared with mountaineering, diving, cave exploring and walking. There are now 11 wetland complexes which have been declared of international importance because of the richness and rarity of their waterfowl and all are protected under the Convention of Ramsar. They could be formed into a league to co-operate in the development of a niche market of European dimensions.

The Area

The Amvrakikos Gulf planning area has a population of approximately 110 000 out of a total of 365 000 inhabitants, living in the three administrative districts where it is constituted. This population increased marginally during the 1970s (+0.8 per cent) in contrast to an overall decline in the three districts. The planning area contains all of the important urban and semi-urban centres in two of the districts: Arta (18 300 inhabitants) and Preveza (12 600), four semi-urban communities (total 15 000), 15 townships (rural centres of between 1 000 and 1 999 inhabitants) as well as 57 communities dispersed among many smaller settlements.

The area surrounding the wetlands (Map A.4) is relatively rich agricultural land supporting primary activities such as pig and poultry farming, fishing and extensive aquaculture (lagoon management) and also agriculture-related industries, including olive processing, cotton mills, fruit juice manufacturing and meat processing facilities. The land also has a rich archaeological and historical heritage with monuments dating back to the Neolithic age and all the way through the prehistoric, ancient Greek, Roman and Byzantine eras to the present day.

Pressure to develop the sensitive environment of the wetlands has been relatively low during the past decade, although there have been public works of irrigation, drainage, land reclamation and river flow regulation for electricity generation. In spite of all of this, the delicate balance of the ecosystem was more or less preserved and its importance as a waterfowl habitat was repeatedly asserted by several studies during the 1980s. But pressure is now mounting, as people become more and more development conscious and oriented. Intensive aquaculture in and around the wetlands was thought of as both the great hope and the great menace at the beginning of the 1980s. The Amvrakikos Programme, however, adopted small-scale schemes which would not alter the ecosystem radically, and only after careful consideration of their environmental consequences. The support of the EC Directorate for the Environment (DG XVI) for this kind of gradual, step by step policy was of crucial importance.

Origin of the Activity

The idea of utilising this valuable environment as an asset for a very moderate kind of tourism (ecological, scientific) came spontaneously and was immediately adopted.

The idea originated in the scientific world and was then initiated by the planning authorities, looking to reinforce the protection of the wetlands against the tendencies to either drain the marshland (sanitation) or over-exploit it through intensive aquaculture. It was hoped that a small but steady stream of visitors would increase local awareness of the ecological value of the wetlands and of the waterfowl. This form of eco-tourism would also help to recompense, to some extent, the social good of the so far preserved wetlands.

The first hint about the value of the area came, of course, from the natural scientists (ichthyologists and ornithologists) who had made detailed surveys and pointed out the biological functions of the double estuary and the lagoons (research groups at the University of Essen in Germany and at Ecoset).

The idea was immediately taken up by the local authorities and approved by local public opinion although, when it came to restrictive measures on the uses of the wetlands (the management plan) some local people were heard to say: "How come these birds are rare! We see them everyday"; or "Why do you put birds before people?"; or "Do you want development to be reduced to bird watching?"

Map A.4. **Amvrakikos Gulf area location in Greece**

The rural people themselves, however, received the idea of eco-tourism more enthusiastically as they felt it would be more beneficial to them than some intensive aquaculture units.

Measures to Create/Sustain the Niche Market

Although there has been continuous interest in and study of the area for more than ten years now, an eco-tourism activity cannot be said to exist yet. Nor is one developing, driven by market forces, to the advantage of the rural people. People studying, filming or otherwise visiting the wetlands do not stay in the nearby villages but gather to spend the evening and their money in the towns.

Thus, if a niche market is to be created for the benefit of the rural population, a positive effort must be made in:

1. Creating some minimum but necessary infrastructure: For those people who are invited to visit the area and who do not come at their own initiative and risk, a minimum of organisation is needed; visitors will otherwise be disappointed and any effort made will be wasted.
2. Developing the necessary expertise amongst the local people. The area has had no tourism until now and, as for eco-tourism, people have little idea what visitors expect, need and appreciate.
3. Reaching out to the market in an attempt to attract the appropriate segment.

To date, all efforts have been concentrated on the first two tasks and active promotion has been left until later.

The following measures have been taken:

1. A ministerial decision has been taken delineating the different zones of the wetlands as protected habitats, with their corresponding permitted land uses and activities. Eco-tourism is one activity allowed under certain conditions. The "decision" was adopted after a long process of study and of discussions with the local authorities, fishermen's cooperatives, business chambers and local people, mainly farmers and hunters.
2. Birds hunting has been suspended in one of the three big lagoons for a two-year period.
3. An international meeting was held in Preveza on the "Management and the Protection of the Wetlands of the Mediterranean", as part of an EC programme, implemented in Greece by the local development agency, ETANAM and the University of Salonika. This is to facilitate the exchange of information and experience.
4. The following have been planned and are now being realised, within the framework of the Community's LEADER Initiative:
   - Rooms for rent will be built in two villages near the lagoons and in one on the Ionian coast.

- A network of bird watching huts will be constructed in appropriate places in collaboration with ornithological groups.
- Walking paths will be maintained and mapped.
- A small natural history museum will be established with the assistance of the Athens Natural History Museum.
- The abandoned railway station and customs buildings at the old harbour of Kopraina in the Gulf will be converted into a small hostel and tavern.
- A camping site will be situated in a wooded area near Preveza, for children's school holidays. Day excursions to the wetlands will be part of their programme.

In conjunction with this, the population is being given advice at various local meetings on what to expect from eco-tourism and on what best to offer the visitors. Later, formal seminars will be organised for the people who intend to run the "rooms to let" and other local businesses. For future consideration are the possibilities of organising guided tours for small groups, using local guides and boatmen, and of offering local fish cuisine, prepared on request by the fishermen at their place of work.

At present, the only information provided is of general interest, through films, leaflets and conferences to scientists, nature lovers and the general public. Those who wish to visit the wetlands have to organise their own excursion. As soon as the necessary infrastructure is in place, the wetlands will be actively promoted. Tourists on the Ionian coast, and people travelling along the main Rio-Arta-Igoumenitsa road will be targeted.

Once enough experience has been gained, a second phase will begin when tourists and visitors will be sought through the trade press and the universities. Currently, the objective is to attract people to the very beautiful but unknown rural area around the wetlands. The wetlands themselves are just one of several attractions to lure them there.

However, eco-tourism would have to be developed to some extent (although the wetlands themselves would be better off without any visitors at all), if the conservation lobby is to be strengthened. Until now, only the hunters' associations have been fighting for the conservation of the moorland as a hunting ground; farmers, on the contrary, would use land reclamation through drainage, and fishermen have been hoping for improvements which would disfigure the landscape and change the hydrological balance of the lagoons; in some cases the fishermen have even tolerated illegal hunting of the waterfowl, including swans, because the birds are known to eat the fish.

The bird life, in conjunction with a well-preserved landscape should act as a source of income for the local people. It should be realised that it is the birds that attract attention and funds to the area and only on the condition that they are protected.

Elements for Success

The most crucial element for the success of the activity is a balanced development of adequate services to support it. For an activity which is market driven, such as hunting in the moorland, there would be no difficulty in achieving this. The expectations of impromptu visitors would be low and the necessary services would develop gradually. However, for an activity which is policy initiated, fine tuning is needed between the different components. These would include: regulation of the use of a fragile environment; the necessary infrastructure; the appropriate attitudes and initiatives of the local people; and the development of demand.

Continuity is also of paramount importance. This kind of tourism is very sensitive and its development is a long-term process. Speed and haste may harm conservation. Thus, continuity is needed to keep the whole effort alive and also to resist pressure to relax protective regulations.

Financing is not a major problem, since the EC finances almost any development initiative and a LEADER programme is specifically designed to support small local initiatives in the rural areas.

The most difficult factor in a non market-driven activity is co-ordination between all the authorities sponsoring it, in particular their achievement of a common understanding and its preservation through continuous changes in personnel.

Constraints on Development

Ecological tourism, by its very nature, has to remain small and limited otherwise it will destroy the resources on which it is based. Nevertheless, if the tourism activity is too limited, it will not be able to sustain the infrastructure nor to fulfil its expectations. The infrastructure will not be properly maintained, as has already been the case at the Prespa lake area in Macedonia, and the initiative will wither. Between these two extremes there is a need for fine tuning by some conscious agency which understands both ecology and economics.

Until now, the Amvrakikos Programme, founded on research by KEPE and continued and implemented by the Ministry of the Environment and ETANAM, has animated the process rather skilfully. However, as already stated a niche market does not exist. Only scientists and ecologists are interested in the area and they only visit it during meetings and conferences. The main beneficiaries are the town hotels and restaurants and the leaflet printers; thus far, fishermen offer boats and guided tours free of charge. It is possible that the birds have benefited from the Programme; 36 couples of the rare and shy ''silver pelican'' have been counted recently, as compared with 12 couples ten years ago.

This is, however, a gestation period. The activity is still new and eco-tourism is very sensitive and imprecisely defined; it includes walks in the marshland, boat tours in the lagoons, bird watching, fish and game cuisine and village festivities. Rural people hesitate to take any initiative or risk apart from traditional village taverns and coffee houses. No great readiness has been manifested to establish other business, except in two villages, one of which is already a summer resort. Lagoon fishermen complain that they do not have time to take visitors around on a regular basis. Nor does any one know yet who will run the ''hostel and tavern'' in the isolated area of Kopraina and for whose benefit. Only the hunters, who envisage it as an ''after hunt'' pavilion, rejoice. But hunting is the one activity that the Programme does not want to foster.

Eco-tourism is clearly difficult to get off the ground. In addition, because the Programme's objective is conservation rather than income generation, it is not being very heavily promoted.

Effects of the Activity on the Rural Area

As noted at the outset, ecological tourism is intended to be only one of several activities aimed at attracting interest and income away from the main tourist areas towards the rural hinterland. Thus, it is the indirect rather than the direct effects that are deemed to be important: the Amvrakikos Gulf has attracted international interest and finance for more than a decade now because of its ecological peculiarities. These features should continue to draw attention to the area and should be either the focus of, or even the pretext for, some kind of activity which is capable of sustaining that interest. It is also hoped that the activity and the interest it generates will strengthen the lobby for conservation and environmental protection. A synergy between the environment and the rural population is thus anticipated.

The effects of such an activity are, of course, not easily quantifiable. The indicator for the most direct effect, the creation of permanent jobs would probably show poor results, given the small size and the length of time taken to develop the activity. Indirect effects are even more difficult to locate, to attribute and to quantify, although research to identify and measure such effects can always be attempted.

In the case of rural economies, where specific measures and policies tend to be small in scale, the effects of each isolated policy are not likely to appear very important. What is important is the impact of a series of measures or policies, implemented concurrently and over a long enough period, on a recognised indicator. The most trustworthy yardstick of the effects of the activity would be to observe the movement of indicators reflecting the economic and social welfare of the area. If the indicators were to show an improvement after an integrated rural policy had been implemented, then that policy may be deemed to be effective and successful.

Population movement could be considered as the most significant indicator but it is usually only measured on a long-term basis, every decade. A comprehensive rural policy cannot be expected to have a permanent impact in a short space of time. Rural economies are small and narrowly based; they are not so flexible that they can react to policies quickly.

According to this last criterion, we can see from Table A4.1 that there is a small increase in the population of the Amvrakikos planning area over the last decade (+4.2 per cent) as against stagnation (+0.8 per cent) and a slight fall (–0.9 per cent) in the previous two decades. This overall increase reflects the growth in population in five out of six "municipalities" and in 46 out of 72 "communities".

The average conceals very different developments in the three sub-areas (Table A4.1), reflecting the diverse natural and socio-economic conditions of the three districts surrounding the Gulf. For each sub-area, though, the improvement in the trend is evident. This improvement cannot, of course, be attributed to the Amvrakikos Programme

Table A4.1. **Evolution of population in the municipalities and communities of the Amvrakikos planning area**

Population changes

	Number of municipalities/ communities	Number of inhabitants				Percentage change		
		1961	1971	1981	1991	1961-71	1971-81	1981-91
Amvrakikos planning area								
Municipalities with more than 3 000 inhabitants	6	45 802	48 579	48 988	51 155	6.06	0.80	4.42
Communities	72	65 209	61 485	61 959	64 451	−5.72	0.77	4.02
Total	78	111 011	110 064	110 944	115 606	−0.86	0.79	4.20
Sub-area belonging to the prefecture of:								
Arta								
Municipalities with more than 3 000 inhabitants	1	17 654	20 538	20 004	20 379	16.33	−2.60	1.87
Communities	39	34 401	32 847	32 594	34 134	−4.52	−0.78	4.72
Total	40	52 055	53 385	52 598	54 513	2.55	−1.48	3.64
Preveza								
Municipalities with more than 3 000 inhabitants	2	15 577	16 032	16 957	18 664	2.92	5.75	10.07
Communities	15	10 277	9 312	10 285	11 313	−9.40	10.44	10.00
Total	17	25 854	25 344	27 242	29 277	−1.97	7.48	10.40
Aitolia-Acarnania								
Municipalities with more than 3 000 inhabitants	3	12 571	12 009	12 007	12 112	−4.47	0.14	0.70
Communities	18	20 531	19 326	19 080	19 004	−5.87	−1.28	−0.40
Total	21	33 102	31 335	31 104	31 116	−5.34	−0.74	0.04

Areas where population increased

	Number of municipalities/communities		
	1961-71	1971-81	1981-91
Amvrakikos planning area			
Municipalities with more than 3 000 inhabitants	5	4	5
Communities	19	28	46
Sub-area belonging to the prefecture of:			
Arta			
Municipalities with more than 3 000 inhabitants	1	1	1
Communities	12	14	23
Preveza			
Municipalities with more than 3 000 inhabitants	2	1	2
Communities	2	8	11
Aitolia-Acarnania			
Municipalities with more than 3 000 inhabitants	2	2	2
Communities	5	6	12

Source: National Statistical Service of Greece, ESYE.

88

nor to any specific local programme; national policies, as well as the regional development policy and the common agricultural policy which was first applied in Greece during this last decade, must have played a crucial role. It is, nevertheless, an indication that after such a strong and comprehensive effort at national, regional and local level, the unfavourable trend of the post war decades has been checked.

The rural context aside, there have been several studies calculating simple and composite economic welfare indices at the administrative district (prefecture) level.[16, 17] However, these cross-sectional studies are appropriate only for inter-regional, not inter-temporal comparisons. For the effects of specific policies to be monitored, such indices should be calculated at regular intervals and be based on regularly surveyed data.

As far as the Amvrakikos area is concerned, there has been no formal attempt to measure the effects of the Programme. Nevertheless, due to existence of this programme, the flow of public and community funds into the area has greatly increased. Construction and tourism activities have also visibly expanded and at least one town, Preveza is becoming an important regional centre for both public and private services (medical, educational, recreational, commercial, welfare). These developments pertain to the promotion and application of the Programme as a whole, not to any one activity. It is the interest generated in the Programme which has fostered and accelerated these developments and this effect is difficult to pin down and quantify.

Assessment

The usefulness of a tourism activity based on an unusual and fragile environment can be assessed as follows:

- this type of tourism activity cannot become very intense; it has to remain modest. Consequently, its impact on rural development will be significant only if it is established either in conjunction with other tourism activities based on alternative attractions or with different activities compatible with the same environment, such as extensive aquaculture. In the case of Amvrakikos, it will affect a very large area only slightly as the wetlands are very extended; its impact will be greater on those villages which may become centres of specific sub-activities;
- it tends to be labour intensive, based on personalised services and minor investments which are likely to make use of the local labour force, in particular for the opening and maintenance of paths, the installation of road signs and bird-watching huts, and for the provision of shelter, catering facilities and guide services. It is an employment generating activity;
- the initial investments required are of a relatively low order, should be of a simple nature and paid in instalments; they can be made by several investors, gradually;
- on the whole, it will not be capable of generating high individual incomes. As the level of activity needs to remain low, labour productivity will also be low. The services offered cannot be priced very high as the people attracted to this kind of tourism, such as students and scientists usually do not have a very high level of income;

89

- however, it is precisely these people who will most probably appreciate the other amenities and commodities in the rural area and provide the impetus for the development of other activities, such as local cuisine, handicrafts and festivals. They also tend to make friends with the local people, thus giving the activity a special character, that of catering for visitors rather than of attending to tourists;
- eco-tourism, by its very nature, facilitates human contact, which is beneficial to tourists and local population alike;
- distinctive environmental features attract specialists from all over and people who have totally different social and economic backgrounds from those who are interested in holiday tourism. Thus a rural area could develop connections unthought of by the usual criteria. Depending on the importance of its distinguishing features, a small area could become a world centre for a particular activity, thereby rescuing it from isolation. The wetlands of Amvrakikos, which have been declared of international importance and which are protected under the Convention of Ramsar, have been visited and studied by several groups from universities, scientific associations, and organisations for the conservation of nature. The surrounding area has also been the subject of several pilot studies and programmes, aimed at combining development with environmental protection.

Policy-making can advance the development of such a niche market:
- by continuously setting a framework and the limits for private activities in the surrounding wetland area, in particular by up-dating the regulations for land and water use, by monitoring the environment and by ensuring that the regulations are respected;
- by helping the rural population to develop marketable goods and services that are associated with the wetlands, such as guided boat tours, footpaths and horse trails across the more interesting parts, bird watching facilities and home-made picnic meals;
- by developing the right spirit among the rural population as regards to eco-tourists. These tourists, although they do not disregard material comforts, tend to give greater value to the genuineness of the natural and cultural environment, the quality of hospitality and food, and cultural pursuits;
- by helping to find and then to approach potentially interested visitors. The National Tourism Organisation, in its effort to develop alternative forms of tourism, could help local promoters locate their target markets and assist them with their promotional activities.

A policy for the development of a niche market is best formulated at the intermediate level of local development agencies, ETANAM for example, where mediation between the rural population and the regional and national authorities can take place. These agencies are usually manned by young scientists who are best suited to combining new ideas, currently emanating from the centres of policy formulation, with knowledge of local conditions and the ways in which the rural people think. They will consequently be able to choose courses of action that have the best prospects for success.

The environment most conducive to the development of such a niche market is one where both the environmental value and the tourist methodology (how to develop a tourist market) have been cultivated for some time. As the Amvrakikos wetland area has had neither tourism nor awareness of an interest in its environment until quite recently, a long period of adaptation has been unavoidable. However, with the encouragement of local initiatives under the LEADER programme and with the existing studies, the development process may be accelerated.

References

ARVANITIS K., GATZELIA A., "Monitoring of the quality of surface waters", Athens, 1990 in *The Amvrakikos Programme,* Vol. 4, KEPE, Report 1.

ECOSET, Athens, "Environmental study for agricultural and aquacultural programmes – Preliminary case study, Amvrakikos, Greece". Final Report, Athens, October 1982.

ETANAM A.E., "Plan for agricultural and eco-tourist development of the Northern Amvrakikos area – Proposition for LEADER Community Initiative", Preveza, August 1991.

GATZELIA A., "Programme of protection and management of the environment", October 1986, in *The Amvrakikos Programme,* Vol. 3, KEPE, Report 1.

GATZELIA A., "Nature reserves and national parks – a proposal for N. Amvrakikos", November 1986, in *The Amvrakikos Programme,* Vol. 4, KEPE.

GATZELIA A., DIMITRIOU D., KOTZABOPOULOS A., "Preliminary programme for the development of alternative forms of tourism", in *The Amvrakikos Programme,* Vol. 3, KEPE.

GOFAS Th., *et al.,* "Feasibility study for fisheries and aquacultural development of the greater Amvrakikos area". Final report, Athens, October 1981.

KAMCHIS M. *et al.,* "Development and protection of the Amvrakikos gulf area". Preliminary report, October 1984, Study for YXOP and CEC (former Ministry of the Environment and the EC).

KOTZABOPOULOS A., "Draft programme for alternative forms of tourism in the north Amvrakikos gulf area", in the *Planning Contract of Amvrakikos,* Ministry of National Economy – EETAA, for the OECD conference on contractual policies for the development of rural areas, Athens-Preveza, May 1988.

PAPAYANNIS Th. *et al.,* "Amvrakikos – Resource development and protection of environment". Final report, September 1985, Study for YXOP and CEC.

PACHAKI C., "Development plan of immediate application", November 1984, in *The Amvrakikòs Programme,* Vol. 1, KEPE.

PACHAKI C., "Mild tourist development", in *The Amvrakikos Programme,* Vol. 2, Chapter 4.2, KEPE.

PACHAKI C., "Planning for an island economy", in the proceedings of the international symposium on island economies, Mytilene, November 1991 (under publication).

UNIVERSITY OF ESSEN, Study group under Prof. Dr. Joseph SZIJJ, "Ecological assessments of the delta area of the rivers Arachtos and Louros at the gulf of Amvrakia", Essen, Germany, 1980.

YPEXODE (Ministry of the Environment), "Delineation study for the wetlands of the Ramsar Convention: Amvrakikos", Athens, 1986.

ZACHARATOS G.A., "Plan of tourist development of the lake Plastira area", KEPE Reports on Planning No. 23, Athens, 1986.

ZALACHORI E., GATZELIA A., "Fisheries development and protection of the lagoons of N. Amvrakikos", November 1986 in *The Amvrakikos Programme,* Vol. 4.

5. The Green Gold of Magnoac – France[18]

The Activity

The starting point of the project was the promotion of a local gastronomic product: foie gras and its preparations. The main objective was to diversify agricultural activities and thereby to maintain the agricultural sector and land management in the area.

As time went on, the strong local image invariably associated with duck and goose products allowed other kinds of local assets to be tapped and exploited on a profitable basis: hiking trails, farmhouses, landscapes and windmills. More generally, the product-territory linkage led to the development of rural tourism and created a residential activity in the form of holiday homes in the region.

The Area

The Magnoac area is the north-eastern part of the Hautes-Pyrénées Department, located on the edge of the Gers and the Haute-Garonne in the Pyrenean foothills, which are less fertile than the lowlands, but less subsidised than the mountain areas (Map A.5). As part of the "Four Valleys Country" which remained independent until 1789, Magnoac consists of two valleys merging southward towards Lannemezan and has long been renowned for its poultry and mule fairs. As it is located in a less favourable area, it receives special assistance from the central government, the regional government, the department and the EC.

Origin of the Activity

With a strong sense of identity, but a markedly ageing and undiversified population of mostly farmers, Magnoac was sinking into a recession when in 1985 a young mayor set up a SIVOM (an intercommunal association with multiple aims), of which he became the chairman. Convinced that his small region did indeed have high-quality natural resources and historical and human assets and the desire to reverse the unfavourable, but by no means irrevocable, economic and population trends, the SIVOM chairman invited

Map A.5.   **Location of Castelnau in France**

Source: DATAR.

the other mayors in Magnoac to undertake an objective review of the territory and its tourism and economic environment.

The mayors drew up a development strategy based on the region's heritage and decided to invest in a pilot project to initiate growth. They compiled a comprehensive report on their area, identifying its weaknesses and assets as follows:

Magnoac's Weaknesses

The ageing of the farming population was closely connected with low farming incomes. It was therefore necessary to increase incomes and to encourage women to stay in the area in order to achieve growth. Table A5.1 compares Castelnau with the rest of rural France, highlighting the agricultural nature of the area, as well as its ageing population.

Magnoac's Assets

South-west France has a traditional gastronomic reputation, especially for duck and goose products which provide a narrow market segment but are high value-added products. It seemed possible to take advantage of the existing local production of ducks and geese as well as foie gras, which had hitherto been sold to outside processing companies.

Table A5.1. **Statistical comparison between Castelnau and rural France**

	Castelnau canton[1]	Rural France[1]
Total population	4 437	..
Population density by km²	21	31
Percentage of communes with less than 200 inhabitants	89.7	35
National migration balance between 1975 and 1982 per year	-1.3	-0.1
Ratio of over 60 to under 20 years old	145	76
Percentage of primary active population	49.7	25.3
Percentage of secondary active population	14.3	33.6
Percentage of migrant	29.7	50
Number of establishment with more than 19 employees	1	..
Percentage of agricultural area in use[2]	61.9	52.6
Percentage of head of household over aged of 55 years old[2]	47.4	45
Percentage of population between 35 and 54 years old with secondary or higher education level	7	9.4

.. not available.
1.   1982 data for France and 1990 data for Castelnau.
2.   Data for rural France refers to whole France.
Source: "Commissariat Général du Plan", France.

The review also identified tourism assets:

- the tradition of holding mule and geese fairs at the small town of Castelnau, which was famous for these events;
- the vicinity of the second biggest tourist centre in France, Lourdes (5 million visitors per year);
- the beauty of the farmland in Magnoac, with small fields separated by hedgerows and trees, as well as the beauty of the farm buildings;
- the large number of tourists travelling through Magnoac year-round on their way to the mountains and to Spain (Magnoac is on the N-E/S-W route to Spain) and the interest of certain tourists, especially from abroad (United Kingdom, Netherlands) in gastronomy made it possible to consider combining the production and promotion of gastronomic products with tourism activities.

Development of the Niche Market

On the basis of this diagnosis, the SIVOM decided to spur local growth by setting up a service for farmers to help them develop local gastronomy by processing and marketing themselves the ducks and geese they were already producing. At the same time, however, it relied on the high quality of the local products and their association with the area of Magnoac, in the promotion of both the products and the territory.

The hope was that this output would improve farm incomes and also make the area known, which in turn would trigger economic growth. Introducing a system allowing farmers to combine foie gras production and tourism activities, provided a way to help them exploit an existing production activity which remained anonymous and did not derive the value-added from processing and marketing, as this was done outside the area. By diversifying the activities of farmers, who tended to concentrate too heavily on maize production, the agricultural sector could be maintained as well as continuing land management practices.

It was also important to reinforce the sense of local identity in a constructive and forward-looking way in order to initiate and develop confidence in the area's future and its capacity to develop. It was then possible to create a strong image combining products with territorial assets to be exploited, such as hiking trails, farmhouses and windmills, and thereby to develop rural tourism and attract a residential population.

A positive image of the area was conveyed to potential public financing bodies at the department, regional, central government and European levels as well as private investors. These sources of financing were encouraged to intervene, with good chances of success.

The SIVOM set up a joint production unit: it first built premises at Castelnau in 1985, then helped producers to set up a CUMA in 1985 (co-operative for the use of agricultural equipment), which purchased the equipment for slaughtering geese and ducks and preparing and packaging foie gras and its derivatives.

The joint production unit procedure was used because it receives a 50 per cent subsidy (22 per cent from central government, 13 per cent from the region and 15 per cent from the department). Originally owned by the SIVOM, the unit will be sold at 50 per cent of its cost (or the part financed by the SIVOM) in 15 years' time to the CUMA, which will acquire it in 2000.

The equipment owned by the CUMA also receives a 50 per cent subsidy, and this is why the programme was selected by the SIVOM (this was the first time it was used for equipment of this type in France).

Elements for Success

The construction of the joint production unit and the creation of the CUMA were the factors that triggered the success of this niche market activity. Since 1985, the production of duck and goose products has grown steadily and at rates compatible with the artisanal production of high quality goods in quantities which enhance the product and territory's image:

- CUMA membership rose from 15 to 42 in eight years;
- the number of ducks and geese slaughtered rose from 4 500 to 25 000 in eight years.

To market its produce, the CUMA has set up a GIE, group of economic interest. The turnover of the GIE has shown a 50 per cent annual growth rate for the past five years. The slaughtering, processing and packaging unit is being extended with EC funding under objective 5b of the LEADER programme. Magnoac was selected because of its dynamism and the image it created in the region.

Foie gras production is developing in France (55 departments currently produce foie gras, seven years after the start of the operations described). Magnoac's marketing policy is therefore more vigorous than at the beginning. The advertising and marketing strategy is focused on "the Green Gold of Magnoac" with the help of a consultancy firm. Promotion and communication funds have increased: FF 600 000 has been provided since 1985 (by FIDAR, the department, region, PDZR and the LEADER programme).

The special quality of the products has been consolidated: importance is given in the advertising to the heat process now being used for evisceration. The product quality specifications, under which aired white maize must be used to feed the ducks and geese, are clearly stated. The range of products is diversified to meet explicit or foreseen demand ("garbure" – a goose soup, "rillettes" – a potted mince).

Initial training of CUMA members by the Institute for the promotion of agricultural and food industries continued and is being more closely targeted. Processing and packaging tools are becoming more efficient and in line with European standards.

Effects of the Activity on the Rural Area

A "Maison du Magnoac" was built in 1988. The "Green Gold of Magnoac" is now increasingly associated with ancillary products: hiking trails, monuments, and accommodation in traditional gîtes. This reflects the solid link between the product and the landscape by expanding tourism activities. Forty-five gîtes have been set up as well as a rural inn and a campsite. A hang-gliding base is being built. New trails have been signposted. A windmill museum incorporating a bakery, where foie gras for immediate consumption will be on offer, is being planned.

A mail order system is being set up for "the Green Gold of Magnoac" products (Magnoac has been included in the department programme for the development of new communication technologies). The mailing list of the "Maison du Magnoac" includes both product consumers and tourists.

There have been spectacular spin-offs from the foie gras niche market in Magnoac compared with the average trends for this type of area in France. The total population has stabilised between the two Census surveys (1982 and 1990) – it has become younger and the number of farming women working at home in duck and goose production has risen. The income of farmers has also increased. New arrivals have settled in the area after purchasing both products and holiday homes, thereby stabilising the population.

The number of empty buildings has dropped. Several have been turned into rental accommodation or gîtes, thereby creating jobs in the construction sector (50 new jobs have been created since 1985). A wood-gilder has set up business, and a sawmill has also been opened, the owner having of his own free will created nine half-time jobs for farmers in difficulty.

Conclusions

The most interesting feature of the Magnoac case is clearly the selection of the gastronomic niche (foie gras, leading to diversification of farming activities and higher farm incomes) but above all the close relationship between niche products, which can be thought of as artisan quality, with a territory having a strong image. This relationship leading to a stronger image or "label" can promote an area making it attractive for economic growth in other sectors, such as tourism. Table A5.2 shows the elements necessary to successfully link this niche product to a territorial image.

The Magnoac experiment has a two-fold advantage:
– through action taken by locally elected representatives, farmers and the area as a whole have had access to a range of tools enabling them to develop this niche market and subsequently to multiply its impact;
– tourism growth leads on to a third phase, involving general economic growth in and around the area as illustrated below.

Traditional Product

↓

Tourism in the area

↓

General growth around the area

↓

Overall growth of the Territory

More than the niche market itself, it is the strategy that has governed its establishment and the tools selected for its growth and that of other activities, that makes this case worth noting.

The activity of the foie gras niche market initiated in 1985, which might have experienced competition problems in spite of its special features, has fully reached its first targets so far, that of ensuring jobs for farmers' wives in the area and the diversification of output and higher incomes. It has also met its second and no doubt longer-term objective of giving Magnoac a high-quality image enabling it to exploit its natural resources and heritage, and ensuring growth.

The role of the foie gras niche is rather like that of a "brand name" in a supermarket (as suggested by the chairman of the SIVOM). It helped to "sell" the territory, which in return has provided a "seal of approval" and label for the product.

Table A5.2. **Success of the niche markets in establishing a territorial image**

1. Territory: Magnoac

A product and know-how and specific gastronomique demand

2. Niche: foie gras

3. Two tools: CUMA and GIE

Associated with the territory, combining:
- land
- men
- a product
- a tool

4. An image – A reputation – Recognition

5. Development

6. Holiday Village in Litschau – Austria[19]

The Activity

Tourist services and the leisure industry have a long tradition in Austria and are of major importance for the national economy. The holiday and seminar village at Litschau, in the Waldviertel region, is an excellent example of an integrated development project which incorporates not just one investment scheme for a single sector but encompasses the entire leisure industry, together with small-scale regional agriculture, trade and industry.

The Litschau project illustrates, in particular, how tourist services can be developed in an unfavourably structured region and demonstrates that success does not depend exclusively on special natural resources, such as healing waters or a glacier area. The Waldviertel has in fact been the subject of continuous and determined efforts by the public authorities to support the area and to transform it from an economically poor region to one rich in services and industry. In 1980, the "Waldviertel Plan" was adopted and supported by a number of funding programmes from the Federal Government and the Province of Lower Austria.

Until the early 1980s, the textile industry dominated the economic structure of Litschau. A crisis in that sector aggravated the existing socio-economic problems of the town; Litschau faced rising unemployment and declining tax revenues, which led to sharply increasing migration. Confronted with this situation, Litschau decided to invest in tourism and make it the leading sector of the economy of the Waldviertel region. On 3 June 1989, the "Farming Village Königsleitn" near Lake Herrensee at Litschau was opened. It was designed for 600 guests with 420 high-quality beds and 180 additional beds.

An infrastructure to support tourism was developed concurrently, with golf courses, tennis and squash courts, a network of hiking and biking routes and rooms for workshops and seminars. The project was entitled "Litschau – a Countryside of Country Sights" (Figure A6.1).

Figure A6.1. **Development concept of holiday village in Litschau**

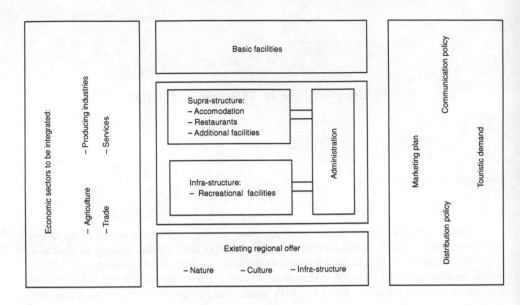

The Area

Litschau is situated in the north of the Waldviertel region in north-eastern Austria and lies next to the formerly closed border between Lower Austria and the Czech Republic (Map A.6). The peripheral position of the Waldviertel with its lack of accessibility for intra- and inter-regional traffic, especially from the major cities of Vienna and Linz, has earned it the label of an unfavourably structured region.

The Waldviertel comprises four administrative districts, centred on the towns of Gmund, Horn, Waidhofen-Thaya and Zwettl and has a population of some 150 000 inhabitants (1991). It is predominantly agricultural, with a mixture of hill farming, pigs and cattle, and forestry but the topography, poor soil and climatic conditions of low and unevenly distributed rainfall restrict agricultural growth. Other traditional activities include timber and wood processing, glass making, breweries, textiles and clothing.

The northern part of the region has experienced severe economic problems; isolated from the centres of economic activity, its communication and transport costs are high and modern services, which are essential for efficient production, are almost non-existent. The level of unemployment is low but this is due to the high levels of migration and

Map A.6. **Litschau area location in Austria**

Source: OECD Secretariat.

commuting outside the area, caused by the continuous loss of employment opportunities in such low-wage industries as clothing and textiles. These industries now face increasing competition from their eastern European neighbours.

An interest in tourist services is developing gradually, concentrated so far on a few towns or areas. The virgin landscape together with a healthy, stimulating climate is considered a promising tourist attraction, ideally suited for "soft-path" tourism (biking, long-distance hiking, horse riding) and offers an alternative to the tourism of the Alpine regions of western Austria, which is both capital-intensive and thought to be harmful to the landscape. The area surrounding Litschau claims to offer enchanting woodlands and other natural sights.

Origin of the Activity

The origin of the Litschau project is dual, in part market-driven as the local conditions were favourable, and in part policy-initiated under the "Waldviertel Plan".

The local authorities at Litschau had decided to invest in tourism and were actively looking for possibilities of attracting tourists. At the same time, a group of local investors was looking for a strong partner to establish a golf course, and large and medium hotel companies were searching for sites in unfavourably structured regions that were as yet unspoiled by excessive development. There was also a growing recognition of the change in emphasis on tourism, towards a more healthy environment for holidays, allowing remedial exercises, relaxation and recovery in natural surroundings away from the beaten track. As a holiday village, Litschau could provide quality accommodation and attract those tourists who sought these attributes without necessarily having to take part in any activity.

The regional and structural problems of the Waldviertel gave rise to a series of initiatives during the 1970s. The Federal Chancellery finally commissioned a study entitled "Proposals for Regional Development in the Waldviertel", later known as the "Waldviertel Plan". The study was drawn up by the Austrian Regional Planning Institute (ÖIR) in co-operation with the Federal and Lower Austrian Governments and with local interest groups. It contained a co-ordinated package of regional policy measures, focusing mainly on trade, industry and tourism but also on agriculture, transport and the infrastructure.

Policies and policy implements which were instrumental in setting up the Litschau project are outlined below:

- The "Special Assistance Campaign for the Creation of Jobs in Trade, Industry and Tourism", established as the first step of the "Waldviertel Plan" and financed by the Federal and Lower Austrian Governments at an annual rate of Sch. 50 million.
- A joint regional special assistance scheme, set up by the Federal and Lower Austrian Governments under the "Waldviertel Plan" with special funding for investment projects, such as tourist establishments. The Litschau project is funded by means of non-repayable subsidies, equivalent to one third of the total investment.
- Loans with favourable rates of interest taken from ERP funds, which are available throughout Austria and are not restricted to projects in the tourist sector; they provided another third of the total investment.
- The appointment of two Regional Advisors for the Waldviertel to help implement the "Waldviertel Plan". The Federal Chancellery appointed one advisor, and the other was selected by the Government of Lower Austria.
- The programme "Aktion 8000", run by the Austrian labour market authority for the creation of jobs for the long-term unemployed and those with little chance of re-employment. The Federal Government covered all direct and indirect salary costs for a two-year period.
- The co-ordination between the local branches of the Chamber of Commerce for Lower Austria and the Regional Managers for the Waldviertel to organise training and further development for local hoteliers and restaurant managers, under a specially-designed programme at a low cost to the participants.
- The hiring of the Austrian Consortium for Independent Regional Development (ÖAR) as part of the Federal Chancellery's "Incentive Programme for Self-Reliant Rural Development", introduced to support innovative economic development projects. Litschau is one of the projects set up under this "regionalisa-

tion'' programme and was designed to maximise the positive effects of the expected rise in tourism in other sectors in the region. The costs were shared by the Federal Chancellery and by the Province of Lower Austria.

Measures to Sustain the Niche Market

The ÖAR, as consultants to the project, were responsible for co-ordinating almost all of the activities at Litschau, with the exception of tour promotions organised by the holiday village operators. Some were "regionalisation" activities, developed especially for the Litschau project. Advisors to the project included the Federal and Lower Austrian Governments, the local authorities, the Chambers of Agriculture and of Commerce and the Austrian Labour Market Authority. Meetings were held two to four times a year.

The project guidelines for the core region around Litschau were designed by the project team, the local authorities and the holiday village operators. The market potential was estimated at Sch 20 million, to be invested both in promoting Litschau as a tourist resort by raising the standards of the tourist organisation and infrastructure, and in integrating the holiday village into the region and the economic sectors (agriculture, trade and industry) into the regionalisation programme.

The first step was to analyse the tourism infrastructure and to evaluate the possible accommodation. The analysis showed that the leisure activities offered and the quality of the rooms available were not up to the standards generally expected by tourists. Neither the people running the tourist information office nor those offering accommodation pursued a professional or systematic approach to marketing.

The initial stage of the Litschau development programme was thus to create a professional tourist organisation, the "Litschau Tourist Service". Now firmly established by the local authorities, it is responsible for providing local tourist information, answering enquiries, co-ordinating and organising leisure activities and for the advertising and public relations. It also provides special services both for the tourists and for all groups and sectors involved in the project. There are five employees, hired by the Austrian Labour Market Authority.

The different members of the project team also had their own responsibilities. These include the following:

- The local authorities simplified and co-ordinated the licensing procedures, helped to develop the infrastructure for the leisure activities and carried out the administrative tasks, such as the registration of tourists and the management of the library, the rent-a-bike service and the photo archives.
- The holiday village operators managed the on-site operation of the holiday village, operated the infrastructure (sports facilities, animation, restaurants, seminar rooms), set up the sales contracts with the tour operators and arranged for international advertising.
- The ÖAR drafted the regionalisation programme, organised the meetings of the advisory group, held seminars to develop the project guidelines, organised the

107

running of the Litschau Tourist Office and trained the employees, designed accommodation packages, and devised the hiking and biking route network.

Elements for Success

The regionalisation programme carried out by the consulting team, from ÖAR, for a period of three and a half years was an essential part of the project. Other important elements considered indispensable for the success of this project were the development of an information network, the setting up of training schemes for the local workforce and the provision of adequate public funding.

From the outset, the project and the existing regional structure, including all sectors of activity, were inter-related. The relevant groups involved were informed whenever a decision concerning the project had to be taken. This not only gave them an opportunity to react to any new developments but also ensured that the follow-up effects on the region could be quickly assessed.

The marketing networks were in place when the holiday village was founded; the investors had already established contact with several tour operators. They launched an advertising campaign at trade fairs and at other promotional events on behalf of the holiday village, keeping the advertising costs to a minimum by pooling the advertising budget of the local authorities with that for the holiday village. A decision was made to market the Litschau region as a single product, the "Waldviertel Area – the healthiest corner of Austria" instead of two separate products, one being the holiday village, and the other the rest of Litschau. Apart from the holiday village folder, various advertising materials were then produced with a standard design and logo; about 30 per cent of the costs were covered by a special scheme for tourism folders.

Several training schemes were devised at Litschau. Excursions for interested persons were arranged to similar holiday villages situated in more favourably structured areas. Employees at already existing holiday villages were then invited to Litschau to work as coaches for the newly employed workforce while those to be later employed at Litschau were sent on training programmes in holiday villages run by the same investor. Further training programmes were organised by the Chamber of Commerce for employees of existing tourist enterprises at Litschau and by the ÖAR for the employees of the Litschau Tourist Service.

The total sum invested in Litschau for establishing the "Farming Village Königsleitn" and for carrying out the regionalisation programme amounted to Sch 212 million. The project was supported by the Federal Government and by the Province of Lower Austria with a subsidy of Sch 70 million. In addition, a loan of Sch 75 million was granted. These sums financed the following investments:

- building and equipment for the holiday village and a number of important infrastructure measures, funded equally from the investor's equity capital, subsidised loans and non-repayable grants;

- consultancy expenses for the holiday village, funded equally by the Federal Government and the Province of Lower Austria;
- building costs of the Tourist Office, funded 50 per cent by both Governments and the provincial Labour Office and 50 per cent by the local authorities; the employment costs are at present paid by the Austrian labour market authority but will in the future be paid by the local authorities.

At the suggestion of the ÖAR consultant, various working groups for specific projects were also formed. They include the restaurant owners, the providers of accommodation and a group named "Health at Litschau" (AGIL) who deal with organising lectures and workshops. A marketing group representing all the organisations and enterprises devised long-term strategies and helped to assist and co-ordinate the activities of the other working groups.

Development: Prerequisites and Constraints

For a niche market activity such as the Litschau project to be successful there are certain essential prerequisites. These include: a minimum of development potential; influential groups or individuals capable of promoting the tourism sector; individuals within the region or outside investors willing to take personal risks and to contribute their know-how; public institutions ready to provide funds and non-financial incentives to overcome the initial drawbacks of an unfavourably structured region; private organisations active in the appropriate sectors to monitor developments. The development process would be constrained if any one of these factors were lacking; if more than one were absent, it may not be able to develop at all.

These potential constraints and how they were successfully avoided at Litschau are itemised as follows:

1. An investor is found but the project gets little support from the local and regional authorities.
   All interested parties were involved from the outset, when negotiations with the investor first took place.
2. No investor can be found who is willing to incur risks in an unfavourably structured region.
   The federal, provincial and local authorities began to contact potential investors at least ten years before the holiday village was opened, at the time the Waldviertel Plan was adopted in 1980.
3. The authorities are unwilling to support the investor as they question the success of the project.
   It was the Waldviertel Plan as well as the efforts of federal and provincial representatives, of the local authorities and of local businesses that made important regional politicians support this plan. The federal and provision authorities were involved at an early stage; they provided funds and non-financial support in implementing the project and meeting formal requirements.

4. The development programme designed for the region is either uni-dimensional or is targeted at an another sector.

The active involvement of the authorities made it possible for almost all the sectors in the holiday project to be inter-related from the start.

5. The tourism sector is too weak for the region to benefit from the activity.

A basic tourism structure was in place at Litschau before the planning stage of the project began. Even though the level of tourist services was below average, the region had products of potential tourist interest.

6. There is little or no co-operation between the different tourist organisations at local and regional levels.

The Tourist Service was founded at the very beginning of the project and is now linked with other tourist structures. Such a service should be a priority for future projects.

7. The main project is heavily promoted; consequently, rival projects are neglected and future co-operation is hindered.

In addition to the holiday village a package of leisure activities, including two golf courses and indoor tennis and squash courts, was negotiated and established at Litschau. The seminar village was added later. Co-ordination was possible as one investor is funding most of the facilities.

8. The labour force in the region is insufficient for the project requirements. Use of outside labour, and also of capital and equipment, does not enhance the value of the region.

In order to obtain and keep qualified staff the management organised training and exchange programmes with other holiday villages.

9. The project is imitated in other, more favourably structured regions and is consequently more likely to succeed.

The authorities ensured that only unfavourably structured regions with a low level of development may benefit from incentive schemes and obtain special funding.

Effects of the Activity

The success of the project is shown by the rising number of beds occupied and by the growth in employment and revenue (Figure A6.2). The project also led to the setting up of other business enterprises, mainly in tourism and trade, making the service sector more important than the producing sectors. The regionalisation programme proved advantageous to the other sectors as well.

By opening a holiday village at Litschau the quality and the quantity of the accommodation improved. The previously existing accommodation is now restructured; a number of standard rooms were converted into luxury accommodation, poor quality rooms were withdrawn. The utilisation of beds offered by professional renters increased both in the holiday village and outside the holiday zone; this has had an effect on the whole region as the Tourist Service sends tourists to hotels in neighbouring areas

Figure A6.2. Holiday village in Litschau

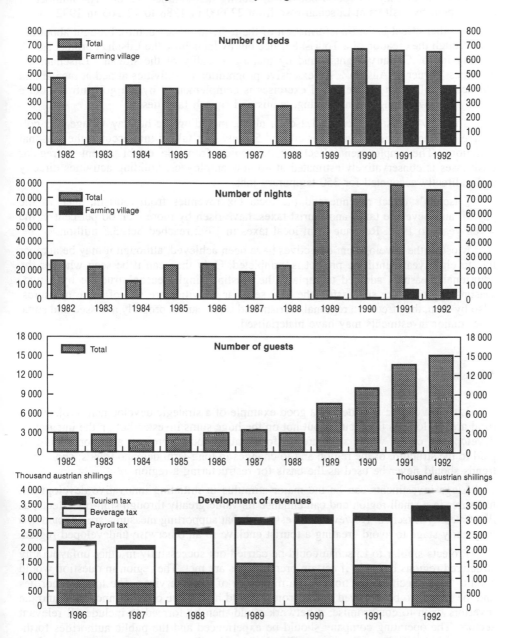

Source: Osterreichisches Statistisches Zentralamt and Litschau Tourist Service.

whenever the holiday village is booked up during the summer season. The number of nights spent by visitors at Litschau rose from 22 600 in 1988 to 72 263 in 1992.

Another effect is the transformation of the tourism infrastructure, brought about not just through the creation of a Tourist Service but by launching the Litschau project as "A countryside of Country Sights" and by making a reality of the slogan "Litschau, the healthiest corner of Austria". An extensive programme of activities aimed at mental and physical equilibrium and remedial exercises is complemented by the golf infrastructure and by the swimming, riding, biking, tennis and squash facilities.

The new tourist services at Litschau alone, including the holiday village, the golf course and the Tourist Service, has created 55 new jobs taking into account the seasonal variations. The employment effect for the region from the establishment of regular businesses is conservatively estimated at 80 new employees; building activities directly and indirectly accounted for 350 temporary jobs.

Litschau's direct revenue and the local tax revenues from tourism, such as the payroll and beverage taxes and tourist taxes, have risen by more than 60 per cent in the seven years to 1992. Revenue from local taxes in 1992 reached Sch 3.5 million.

Most of the development objectives have been achieved, although it may be another five to eight years until the project is completed. Only then can it be seen whether the additional measures adopted to replace the existing single-season structure by a two-seasons approach are successful; the new seminar activities are one of these measures. Also by then, the effects on regional tourism and trade can be properly assessed and some other major investments may have materialised.

Assessment

Litschau can be regarded as a good example of a strategic development project in a rural area as long as the focus is put not on the huge sums invested but on the integrative development of the whole structure. In formulating such a project, attention should be paid to the structure of the region and to changes in long-term demand trends; short-term trends should never be used as the basis for restructuring a region.

Large investments can be the major stimulus in initiating innovative development measures in a small region and can enhance its value greatly through spin-off effects, as illustrated by Litschau. However, it is essential that supporting measures are adopted at a very early stage to avoid creating a tourist enclave in an otherwise undeveloped region.

Projects similar to Litschau could be carried out successfully in other unfavourably structured regions but only if certain prerequisites are met. The region in question would need to have specific attractions and a minimum of basic services. The local authorities and the groups to be involved in the project would have to be open to innovation and the investors open to compromise; a network could then be formed to include all relevant sectors. The operating company should be experienced and the public authorities forthcoming with a funding programme. Finally, a regional management team or consultant should remain on site and in the surrounding area to provide advice.

Similar projects elsewhere in Austria have been successful, particularly in Styria, Carinthia and the Burgenland; the investor for Litschau is currently planning an even larger tourist project in the Styrian Eisenstrasse region, to be implemented by 1995. The concept of self-reliant regional development will also be applied there. In fact, a regional policy is essential to combat the disadvantages; without one, such projects in poorly developed and unfavourably structured regions would fail.

Notes and References

1. *What Future for Our Countryside? A Rural Development Policy,* OECD Publication, Paris, 1993.
2. For example: *Agricultural Policies, Markets and Trade: Monitoring and Outlook 1988-93,* OECD Publication, Paris, 1988-93.
3. *Marketing Strategy: A Customer-Driven Approach,* Steaven P. Schnaars, The Free Press, 1991.
4. *Competitive Advantage,* Michael E. Porter, The Free Press, 1985.
5. *Economics (8th Edition),* R.G. Lipsey, P.O. Steiner, D.D. Purvis, Harper and Row, 1987.
6. *Market Segmentation, Product Differentiation, and Marketing Strategy,* P.R. Dickson and J.L. Ginter, *Journal of Marketing,* April 1987.
7. *Fundamentals of Marketing (9th Edition),* W.J. Stanton, M.J. Etzel, B.J. Walker, McGraw-Hill, Inc., 1991.
8. *Implementing Change: Entrepreneurship and Local Initiative,* OECD Publication, Paris, 1990.
9. *Education for Entrepreneurship,* W. During, New Findings and Perspectives in Entrepreneurship (edited by R. Donckels and A. Miettinen), Avebury, 1990.
10. *Règlement (CEE) No. 2081/92 du Conseil* du 14 juillet 1992, Journal Officiel des Communautés Européennes, 1992.
11. This case study was prepared by Mr. Tsutomu Aoki, Ministry of Agriculture, Forestry and Fisheries, Tokyo, Japan.
12. This case study was prepared by Mr. Per Ofstad, Ministry of Agriculture, Oslo, Norway.
13. "Duodji" is a special feature of Sami culture, an aesthetic form of handicraft that is expressed differently from area to area. The products are functional and reflect local traditions and are made from wood, bone and reindeer hides. The leather products include purses, jewellery and watchbands, some of which are decorated with pewter thread embroidery.
14. This case study was prepared by Prof. Donald Reid, Ms. Kerry Knowles and Mr. Craig Teal, University of Guelph, Canada.
15. This case study was prepared by Ms. Calliope Pachaki, Centre of Planning and Economic Research, Athens, Greece.
16. *KEPE Reports on Planning No. 24,* "Basic data by district and region", E. Theodori-Marcoyannaki *et al.,* Athens, 1986.
17. *KEPE Studies No. 40,* "Indices of regional development in Greece", P.A. Kavvadias, Athens, 1992.
18. This case study was prepared by Ms. Christine Kovacshazy, Commissariat Général du Plan, Paris, France.
19. This case study was prepared by Dr. Wolfgang Sovis, ÖAR Regionalberatung Gesmbh Waldviertel-Weinviertel, Austria.

MAIN SALES OUTLETS OF OECD PUBLICATIONS
PRINCIPAUX POINTS DE VENTE DES PUBLICATIONS DE L'OCDE

ARGENTINA – ARGENTINE
Carlos Hirsch S.R.L.
Galería Güemes, Florida 165, 4° Piso
1333 Buenos Aires   Tel. (1) 331.1787 y 331.2391
Telefax: (1) 331.1787

AUSTRALIA – AUSTRALIE
D.A. Information Services
648 Whitehorse Road, P.O.B 163
Mitcham, Victoria 3132   Tel. (03) 873.4411
Telefax: (03) 873.5679

AUSTRIA – AUTRICHE
Gerold & Co.
Graben 31
Wien I   Tel. (0222) 533.50.14

BELGIUM – BELGIQUE
Jean De Lannoy
Avenue du Roi 202
B-1060 Bruxelles   Tel. (02) 538.51.69/538.08.41
Telefax: (02) 538.08.41

CANADA
Renouf Publishing Company Ltd.
1294 Algoma Road
Ottawa, ON K1B 3W8   Tel. (613) 741.4333
Telefax: (613) 741.5439
Stores:
61 Sparks Street
Ottawa, ON K1P 5R1   Tel. (613) 238.8985
211 Yonge Street
Toronto, ON M5B 1M4   Tel. (416) 363.3171
Telefax: (416)363.59.63
Les Éditions La Liberté Inc.
3020 Chemin Sainte-Foy
Sainte-Foy, PQ G1X 3V6   Tel. (418) 658.3763
Telefax: (418) 658.3763

Federal Publications Inc.
165 University Avenue, Suite 701
Toronto, ON M5H 3B8   Tel. (416) 860.1611
Telefax: (416) 860.1608
Les Publications Fédérales
1185 Université
Montréal, QC H3B 3A7   Tel. (514) 954.1633
Telefax : (514) 954.1635

CHINA – CHINE
China National Publications Import
Export Corporation (CNPIEC)
16 Gongti E. Road, Chaoyang District
P.O. Box 88 or 50
Beijing 100704 PR   Tel. (01) 506.6688
Telefax: (01) 506.3101

CZECH REPUBLIC – RÉPUBLIQUE TCHÈQUE
Artia Pegas Press Ltd.
Narodni Trida 25
POB 825
111 21 Praha 1   Tel. 26.65.68
Telefax: 26.20.81

DENMARK – DANEMARK
Munksgaard Book and Subscription Service
35, Nørre Søgade, P.O. Box 2148
DK-1016 København K   Tel. (33) 12.85.70
Telefax: (33) 12.93.87

EGYPT – ÉGYPTE
Middle East Observer
41 Sherif Street
Cairo   Tel. 392.6919
Telefax: 360-6804

FINLAND – FINLANDE
Akateeminen Kirjakauppa
Keskuskatu 1, P.O. Box 128
00100 Helsinki
Subscription Services/Agence d'abonnements :
P.O. Box 23
00371 Helsinki   Tel. (358 0) 12141
Telefax: (358 0) 121.4450

FRANCE
OECD/OCDE
Mail Orders/Commandes par correspondance:
2, rue André-Pascal
75775 Paris Cedex 16   Tel. (33-1) 45.24.82.00
Telefax: (33-1) 49.10.42.76
Telex: 640048 OCDE
Orders via Minitel, France only/
Commandes par Minitel, France exclusivement :
36 15 OCDE

OECD Bookshop/Librairie de l'OCDE :
33, rue Octave-Feuillet
75016 Paris   Tel. (33-1) 45.24.81.67
(33-1) 45.24.81.81
Documentation Française
29, quai Voltaire
75007 Paris   Tel. 40.15.70.00
Gibert Jeune (Droit-Économie)
6, place Saint-Michel
75006 Paris   Tel. 43.25.91.19
Librairie du Commerce International
10, avenue d'Iéna
75016 Paris   Tel. 40.73.34.60
Librairie Dunod
Université Paris-Dauphine
Place du Maréchal de Lattre de Tassigny
75016 Paris   Tel. (1) 44.05.40.13
Librairie Lavoisier
11, rue Lavoisier
75008 Paris   Tel. 42.65.39.95
Librairie L.G.D.J. - Montchrestien
20, rue Soufflot
75005 Paris   Tel. 46.33.89.85
Librairie des Sciences Politiques
30, rue Saint-Guillaume
75007 Paris   Tel. 45.48.36.02
P.U.F.
49, boulevard Saint-Michel
75005 Paris   Tel. 43.25.83.40
Librairie de l'Université
12a, rue Nazareth
13100 Aix-en-Provence   Tel. (16) 42.26.18.08
Documentation Française
165, rue Garibaldi
69003 Lyon   Tel. (16) 78.63.32.23
Librairie Decitre
29, place Bellecour
69002 Lyon   Tel. (16) 72.40.54.54

GERMANY – ALLEMAGNE
OECD Publications and Information Centre
August-Bebel-Allee 6
D-53175 Bonn   Tel. (0228) 959.120
Telefax: (0228) 959.12.17

GREECE – GRÈCE
Librairie Kauffmann
Mavrokordatou 9
106 78 Athens   Tel. (01) 32.55.321
Telefax: (01) 36.33.967

HONG-KONG
Swindon Book Co. Ltd.
13–15 Lock Road
Kowloon, Hong Kong   Tel. 2376.2062
Telefax: 2376.0685

HUNGARY – HONGRIE
Euro Info Service
Margitsziget, Európa Ház
1138 Budapest   Tel. (1) 111.62.16
Telefax : (1) 111.60.61

ICELAND – ISLANDE
Mál Mog Menning
Laugavegi 18, Pósthólf 392
121 Reykjavik   Tel. 162.35.23

INDIA – INDE
Oxford Book and Stationery Co.
Scindia House
New Delhi 110001   Tel.(11) 331.5896/5308
Telefax: (11) 332.5993
17 Park Street
Calcutta 700016   Tel. 240832

INDONESIA – INDONÉSIE
Pdii-Lipi
P.O. Box 4298
Jakarta 12042   Tel. (21) 573.34.67
Telefax: (21) 573.34.67

IRELAND – IRLANDE
Government Supplies Agency
Publications Section
4/5 Harcourt Road
Dublin 2   Tel. 661.31.11
Telefax: 478.06.45

ISRAEL
Praedicta
5 Shatner Street
P.O. Box 34030
Jerusalem 91430   Tel. (2) 52.84.90/1/2
Telefax: (2) 52.84.93
R.O.Y.
P.O. Box 13056
Tel Aviv 61130   Tél. (3) 49.61.08
Telefax (3) 544.60.39

ITALY – ITALIE
Libreria Commissionaria Sansoni
Via Duca di Calabria 1/1
50125 Firenze   Tel. (055) 64.54.15
Telefax: (055) 64.12.57
Via Bartolini 29
20155 Milano   Tel. (02) 36.50.83
Editrice e Libreria Herder
Piazza Montecitorio 120
00186 Roma   Tel. 679.46.28
Telefax: 678.47.51
Libreria Hoepli
Via Hoepli 5
20121 Milano   Tel. (02) 86.54.46
Telefax: (02) 805.28.86
Libreria Scientifica
Dott. Lucio de Biasio 'Aeiou'
Via Coronelli, 6
20146 Milano   Tel. (02) 48.95.45.52
Telefax: (02) 48.95.45.48

JAPAN – JAPON
OECD Publications and Information Centre
Landic Akasaka Building
2-3-4 Akasaka, Minato-ku
Tokyo 107   Tel. (81.3) 3586.2016
Telefax: (81.3) 3584.7929

KOREA – CORÉE
Kyobo Book Centre Co. Ltd.
P.O. Box 1658, Kwang Hwa Moon
Seoul   Tel. 730.78.91
Telefax: 735.00.30

MALAYSIA – MALAISIE
University of Malaya Bookshop
University of Malaya
P.O. Box 1127, Jalan Pantai Baru
59700 Kuala Lumpur
Malaysia   Tel. 756.5000/756.5425
Telefax: 756.3246

MEXICO – MEXIQUE
Revistas y Periodicos Internacionales S.A. de C.V.
Florencia 57 - 1004
Mexico, D.F. 06600   Tel. 207.81.00
Telefax : 208.39.79

NETHERLANDS – PAYS-BAS
SDU Uitgeverij Plantijnstraat
Externe Fondsen
Postbus 20014
2500 EA's-Gravenhage   Tel. (070) 37.89.880
Voor bestellingen: Telefax: (070) 34.75.778

**NEW ZEALAND
NOUVELLE-ZÉLANDE**
Legislation Services
P.O. Box 12418
Thorndon, Wellington   Tel. (04) 496.5652
                            Telefax: (04) 496.5698

NORWAY – NORVÈGE
Narvesen Info Center – NIC
Bertrand Narvesens vei 2
P.O. Box 6125 Etterstad
0602 Oslo 6   Tel. (022) 57.33.00
                   Telefax: (022) 68.19.01

PAKISTAN
Mirza Book Agency
65 Shahrah Quaid-E-Azam
Lahore 54000   Tel. (42) 353.601
                    Telefax: (42) 231.730

PHILIPPINE – PHILIPPINES
International Book Center
5th Floor, Filipinas Life Bldg.
Ayala Avenue
Metro Manila   Tel. 81.96.76
                    Telex 23312 RHP PH

PORTUGAL
Livraria Portugal
Rua do Carmo 70-74
Apart. 2681
1200 Lisboa   Tel.: (01) 347.49.82/5
                   Telefax: (01) 347.02.64

SINGAPORE – SINGAPOUR
Gower Asia Pacific Pte Ltd.
Golden Wheel Building
41, Kallang Pudding Road, No. 04-03
Singapore 1334   Tel. 741.5166
                      Telefax: 742.9356

SPAIN – ESPAGNE
Mundi-Prensa Libros S.A.
Castelló 37, Apartado 1223
Madrid 28001   Tel. (91) 431.33.99
                    Telefax: (91) 575.39.98

Libreria Internacional AEDOS
Consejo de Ciento 391
08009 – Barcelona   Tel. (93) 488.30.09
                         Telefax: (93) 487.76.59
Llibreria de la Generalitat
Palau Moja
Rambla dels Estudis, 118
08002 – Barcelona
        (Subscripcions) Tel. (93) 318.80.12
        (Publicacions) Tel. (93) 302.67.23
                Telefax: (93) 412.18.54

SRI LANKA
Centre for Policy Research
c/o Colombo Agencies Ltd.
No. 300-304, Galle Road
Colombo 3   Tel. (1) 574240, 573551-2
                 Telefax: (1) 575394, 510711

SWEDEN – SUÈDE
Fritzes Information Center
Box 16356
Regeringsgatan 12
106 47 Stockholm   Tel. (08) 690.90.90
                        Telefax: (08) 20.50.21

Subscription Agency/Agence d'abonnements :
Wennergren-Williams Info AB
P.O. Box 1305
171 25 Solna   Tel. (08) 705.97.50
                    Téléfax : (08) 27.00.71

SWITZERLAND – SUISSE
Maditec S.A. (Books and Periodicals - Livres
et périodiques)
Chemin des Palettes 4
Case postale 266
1020 Renens VD 1   Tel. (021) 635.08.65
                        Telefax: (021) 635.07.80

Librairie Payot S.A.
4, place Pépinet
CP 3212
1002 Lausanne   Tel. (021) 341.33.47
                     Telefax: (021) 341.33.45

Librairie Unilivres
6, rue de Candolle
1205 Genève   Tel. (022) 320.26.23
                   Telefax: (022) 329.73.18

Subscription Agency/Agence d'abonnements :
Dynapresse Marketing S.A.
38 avenue Vibert
1227 Carouge   Tel.: (022) 308.07.89
                    Telefax : (022) 308.07.99

See also – Voir aussi :
OECD Publications and Information Centre
August-Bebel-Allee 6
D-53175 Bonn (Germany)   Tel. (0228) 959.120
                        Telefax: (0228) 959.12.17

TAIWAN – FORMOSE
Good Faith Worldwide Int'l. Co. Ltd.
9th Floor, No. 118, Sec. 2
Chung Hsiao E. Road
Taipei   Tel. (02) 391.7396/391.7397
              Telefax: (02) 394.9176

THAILAND – THAÏLANDE
Suksit Siam Co. Ltd.
113, 115 Fuang Nakhon Rd.
Opp. Wat Rajbopith
Bangkok 10200   Tel. (662) 225.9531/2
                     Telefax: (662) 222.5188

TURKEY – TURQUIE
Kültür Yayinlari Is-Türk Ltd. Sti.
Atatürk Bulvari No. 191/Kat 13
Kavaklidere/Ankara   Tel. 428.11.40 Ext. 2458
Dolmabahce Cad. No. 29
Besiktas/Istanbul   Tel. 260.71.88
                         Telex: 43482B

UNITED KINGDOM – ROYAUME-UNI
HMSO
Gen. enquiries   Tel. (071) 873 0011
Postal orders only:
P.O. Box 276, London SW8 5DT
Personal Callers HMSO Bookshop
49 High Holborn, London WC1V 6HB
                Telefax: (071) 873 8200
Branches at: Belfast, Birmingham, Bristol, Edin-
burgh, Manchester

UNITED STATES – ÉTATS-UNIS
OECD Publications and Information Centre
2001 L Street N.W., Suite 700
Washington, D.C. 20036-4910 Tel. (202) 785.6323
                        Telefax: (202) 785.0350

VENEZUELA
Libreria del Este
Avda F. Miranda 52, Aptdo. 60337
Edificio Galipán
Caracas 106   Tel. 951.1705/951.2307/951.1297
                   Telegram: Libreste Caracas

Subscription to OECD periodicals may also be
placed through main subscription agencies.

Les abonnements aux publications périodiques de
l'OCDE peuvent être souscrits auprès des
principales agences d'abonnement.

Orders and inquiries from countries where Distribu-
tors have not yet been appointed should be sent to:
OECD Publications Service, 2 rue André-Pascal,
75775 Paris Cedex 16, France.

Les commandes provenant de pays où l'OCDE n'a
pas encore désigné de distributeur peuvent être
adressées à : OCDE, Service des Publications,
2, rue André-Pascal, 75775 Paris Cedex 16, France.

1-1995

OECD PUBLICATIONS, 2 rue André-Pascal, 75775 PARIS CEDEX 16
PRINTED IN FRANCE
(04 95 03 1) ISBN 92-64-14390-4 - No. 47779 1995